CHARLES RENNIE MACKINTOSH IN FRANCE

PAMELA ROBERTSON
& PHILIP LONG

CHARLES RENNIE MACKINTOSH IN FRANCE

LANDSCAPE WATERCOLOURS

NATIONAL GALLERIES OF SCOTLAND · 2005
IN COLLABORATION WITH THE HUNTERIAN ART GALLERY
UNIVERSITY OF GLASGOW

Published by the Trustees
of the National Galleries of Scotland
in collaboration with the Hunterian Art Gallery,
University of Glasgow, to accompany the exhibition
Charles Rennie Mackintosh in France: Landscape Watercolours
held at the Dean Gallery, Edinburgh from
26 November 2005 to 5 February 2006.

ISBN 1 903278 71 6

Designed by Dalrymple
Typeset in Collis and Penumbra
Printed in Belgium by Die Keure

Front cover: detail from C.R. Mackintosh *La Rue du Soleil* [plate 16]
Hunterian Art Gallery, University of Glasgow

Back cover: C.R. Mackintosh *Mimosa, Amélie-les-Bains* [plate 39]
Hunterian Art Gallery, University of Glasgow

Frontispiece: detail from C.R. Mackintosh *Mont Alba* [plate 5]
Scottish National Gallery of Modern Art,
Edinburgh

SPONSOR'S PREFACE

Deloitte.

Deloitte is honoured to have the opportunity to demonstrate the firm's continuous support for the arts in Scotland by sponsoring this prestigious exhibition of the works of one of the country's most celebrated artists.

Through a series of rarely seen landscape watercolours and personal letters, this exhibition provides a unique insight into the latter years of the life of Charles Rennie Mackintosh.

We look forward to sharing this magnificent opportunity with our clients, our people and the Scottish public. We do hope you enjoy the exhibition.

ROBERT WILSON
Partner, Deloitte

FOREWORD

Towards the end of his life, the innovative Scottish architect and designer, Charles Rennie Mackintosh, gave up his career and moved to the south of France. There, between 1923 and 1927, he concentrated exclusively on painting the area around Port Vendres and the countryside between that Mediterranean port and the small town of Mont Louis in the French Pyrénées. The exceptional group of watercolours he produced represents the sole artistic output of his last years. Few of these works were seen publicly until the *Mackintosh Memorial Exhibition*, held in Glasgow in 1933.

Although in recent years a number of exhibitions have examined Mackintosh's career, there has not been a comprehensive attempt to bring together these late watercolours since the large-scale exhibition of his works on paper organised by Glasgow Museums in 1978. Since then, a number of the French paintings, believed lost, have been rediscovered (although a few remain missing). In 2001 the University of Glasgow, the holders of Mackintosh's estate, made the important decision to publish Mackintosh's letters to his wife, Margaret Macdonald, written from the south of France between May and June 1927. These comprise one of the very few original documents to exist in Mackintosh's hand and are of great importance. Since this focused attention on Mackintosh's concerns and working methods during that period, an exhibition of the related paintings seemed timely. More recently, three further letters have emerged, written by Margaret Macdonald Mackintosh at the beginning of the couple's stay in France. These throw new light on their early time there and are published here in full for the first time.

This exhibition has been a productive collaboration between the National Galleries of Scotland and the Hunterian Art Gallery, University of Glasgow. We are indebted to Mungo Campbell, deputy director, and in particular to Pamela Robertson, senior curator at the Gallery and Professor of Mackintosh Studies at the University of Glasgow, for their support and advice throughout the development of the project. The exhibition has been co-curated by Pamela Robertson and Philip Long, senior curator at the Scottish National Gallery of Modern Art, who has undertaken the principal organisation. The production of this accompanying catalogue, with informative essays by Pamela Robertson and Philip Long, has been seen through production by Christine Thompson and David Simpson of the National Galleries of Scotland's Publishing Department. Space does not allow individual mention of the numerous other Gallery staff who have contributed and to whom we are grateful.

In addition to the Hunterian Art Gallery, which has lent over forty works from its unrivalled Mackintosh collection, we are indebted to those other institutions who have generously agreed to lend to the exhibition, including The Art Institute of Chicago, The British Museum, Glasgow Museums and Galleries, Glasgow School of Art, National Library of Dublin, National Trust for Scotland, and Tate. We are also extremely grateful to Donald and Eleanor Taffner and the many other private collectors who wish to remain anonymous. We would also like to thank the following who have helped towards the preparation of the exhibition and catalogue in various ways: Chris Allan, Robin Barlow, Roger Billcliffe, Patrick Bourne, Bernard Catllar, Robin and Flora Crichton, Professor Jim Dickson, Shirley-Anne Fowlie, William Hardie, Susie Nichol, Hiroko Onoda, Pilar Ordovás, Andrew McIntosh Patrick, Peter Trowles, Emily Walsh, and Bernard Williams.

Finally, we are very grateful to Deloitte for their generous sponsorship of the exhibition, the first at the National Galleries of Scotland to be devoted to this outstanding architect, designer and artist.

SIR TIMOTHY CLIFFORD
Director-General, National Galleries of Scotland

RICHARD CALVOCORESSI
Director, Scottish National Gallery of Modern Art

Fig.1 | *Charles Rennie Mackintosh and Margaret Macdonald Mackintosh Memorial Exhibition*, McLellan Galleries, Glasgow 1933. The four French landscapes are, clockwise from top left, *The Rock* [plate 28], *Port Vendres* [plate 27], *Bouleternère* [plate 2] and *Collioure* [plate 11].

MACKINTOSH'S FRENCH WATERCOLOURS

PAMELA ROBERTSON

Today Charles Rennie Mackintosh (1868–1928) is celebrated worldwide as one of the most creative and individual architect-designers of the 1890s and early 1900s [fig.2]. His achievements are promoted in international exhibitions and publications, and his works fetch world-record prices at auction. Such acclaim was not achieved in Mackintosh's lifetime, and he spent the final four years of his life in quiet seclusion in the south of France, with his wife, Margaret Macdonald (1864–1933) [fig.3]. There, he devoted himself to painting, producing a series of some forty watercolours depicting mountain landscapes, farm buildings, hill towns, ports and flowers. The watercolours are both highly sophisticated compositions and also important documents. In the absence of other evidence, they provide a valuable visual diary of the couple's final years together, and resonant testimony to Mackintosh's mastery of the watercolour medium.

BEFORE FRANCE: ARCHITECT & DESIGNER

Mackintosh's career before his departure for France in 1923 was centred on his native Glasgow, and was dominated by his achievements as an architect and designer. He trained at Glasgow School of Art from 1884, and joined one of the city's leading architectural practices, Honeyman & Keppie, as an apprentice in 1889, becoming a partner in 1901. As a student in the 1890s, he travelled widely in Scotland and England, absorbing the forms and materials of traditional Scottish architecture and investigating the progressive ideas of the English Arts and Crafts movement. His first buildings date from the mid-1890s and include premises for the *Glasgow Herald* newspaper (1893–5), Martyrs' School (1895–8) and Queen's Cross Church (1897–9). His masterpiece, the Glasgow School of Art, was begun at this time and completed a decade later (1897–9; 1907–9) [fig.4]. The early 1900s were intensely productive and included the design of Windyhill (1900–1), the *Daily Record* building (1900–2), The Hill House, in nearby Helensburgh (1902–4), and Scotland Street School (1903–6). In common with other leading architects of the day, Mackintosh saw the architect as being responsible not just for the fabric but for the complete design of a building, including furniture, fixtures and decorative schemes. As a designer he was one of the leading exponents of the concept of the room as a work of art, creating at The Hill House and notably at a series of city-centre tea rooms, interiors of a rarefied decorative and symbolic beauty, set with furniture, often of breathtaking formal sophistication [figs.5 & 6].

In 1900 he married Margaret Macdonald, one of the most gifted women artists of the period, and she became his artistic collaborator, lifelong companion and soulmate. Mackintosh's work, frequently with that of his Glasgow contemporaries, was widely exhibited from the late 1890s to the early 1900s, in Paris, London, Venice, Vienna, Darmstadt, Turin, and elsewhere, and published in the leading British and Continental periodicals of the day. While many commentators were puzzled by the new Glasgow work, most acknowledged its adventurous and distinctive character, and some recognised its importance. The perceptive German critic Hermann Muthesius concluded, 'If one were to go through the list of truly original artists, the creative minds of the modern movement, the name of Charles Rennie Mackintosh would certainly be included amongst the few that one can count on the fingers of one hand.'[1]

By 1909 circumstances had changed. An economic downturn in Glasgow, combined with changing architectural taste in favour of classicism, contributed to Mackintosh's departure from Honeyman, Keppie & Mackintosh. He failed to set up an independent practice, and in 1914, the Mackintoshes left Glasgow for a recuperative break in Walberswick, Suffolk, a break that extended to fifteen months due to the outbreak of the First World War. From there they moved to London. Though the couple soon formed part of a lively artistic group in Chelsea, Mackintosh was not successful in establishing a viable practice in the city. Wartime restrictions severely curtailed new work. In his eight years in the capital, Mackintosh's executed architectural and design work comprised: remodelling and part furnishing of a terrace house in Northampton and related minor commissions in the area, one studio in Chelsea, the modest extension of a house in East Grinstead and alterations to cottages in Sussex. There was no upturn after the war and no completed design work after 1920 is known. Though Mackintosh had some success with commercial textile design, income and prospects were limited. By the summer of 1923, the couple decided on a major change, to leave England for France, and to concentrate on watercolour painting. Doubtless they were encouraged to consider moving to France by their good friends the Scottish painter, J.D. Fergusson (1874–1961) and his partner, the dancer, Margaret Morris. Fergusson and Morris had spent idyllic and productive periods together in the Alpes Maritimes before and after the First World War. Further encouragement would have come from the young English artists, Rudolph Ihlee (1883–1968) and Edgar Hereford (c.1884–1930) whom the Mackintoshes knew in Chelsea and who had moved to Collioure, France, by 1922 [fig.7].

It was rare for an architect to develop a parallel career as an artist, but Mackintosh had had a lifelong interest in drawing, painting and graphic design. In his immediate Glasgow circle he had several role models of professionals who also painted and exhibited. His senior partner, John Keppie, regularly showed topographical watercolours at the Glasgow Institute. Francis Newbery, Director of Glasgow School of Art from 1885 to 1917, was a prolific painter who exhibited in England and Scotland, and on the Continent. And his closest associates from the 1890s, Herbert McNair and Margaret and Frances Macdonald, were also designers and makers of objects, as well as gifted painters.

'A ROSE-COLOURED LAND'

The French Pyrénées and the Roussillon coast were not fashionable destinations in the early 1920s. None the less, a small body of enthusiastic writings by R.L. Stevenson, Hillaire Belloc and others, many of them illustrated, extolled its virtues for climbing, walking, seclusion, and unspoilt nature and local architecture.[2] The summer flora 'rivalled that of the Alps' and Canigou, the landmark mountain, was 'a magician among mountains'.[3] Macdonald read at least one such text, an enthusiastic account by the American Amy Oakley, illustrated by her husband, Thornton Oakley [fig.8]. Macdonald's notes from it survive, suggesting the Mackintoshes considered visiting the Spanish Basque country.[4] In 1923, the couple let their London studios, packed a few belongings, and set off on the long journey by ferry and rail for the south of France.

Establishing a chronology for the subsequent four years in France is difficult, as only a few of the watercolours are dated: *Mimosa, Amélie-les-Bains*, 1924; a group of four flowers drawings, from Mont Louis, all dated 1925; *La Rue du Soleil*, Port Vendres, dated twice – 1926 and 1927; *Le Fort Maillert, The Little Bay* and *The Rock*, all Port Vendres, 1927. Other destinations documented by the watercolours include the fishing village of Collioure, the valley towns of Ille-sur-Têt, Palalda and Bouleternère, and the mountain villages of Fetges and La Llagonne. It seems probable that by 1925 the Mackintoshes had established a routine of summering in Mont Louis, and spending the rest of the year on the coast at Port Vendres. What is clear is that the Mackintoshes preferred to stay in smaller, less fashionable spots. Cost and the wish for tranquillity, having abandoned the big urban centres of Glasgow and London, certainly would have been considerations, but the couple also had a clear delight in the honest and unpretentious. Such tastes were reflected in Mackintosh's choice of subjects for his watercolours. Other visits were made, possibly to Spain and certainly to Patrick Geddes in Montpellier.[5]

Apart from the watercolours, the principal source for documenting the years in France are the few surviving letters written by the

couple. These comprise two well-known letters from Mackintosh to J.D. Fergusson (1 February 1925, Ille-sur-Têt) and Francis Newbery, (28 December 1925, Port Vendres), and the series of twenty-three long letters dubbed 'The Chronycle', written by Mackintosh to Macdonald from Port Vendres in the early summer of 1927 when she was temporarily in London for medical reasons.[6]

Recently three letters from Macdonald to her close friend, the artist Jessie Newbery, wife of Francis Newbery, have emerged [fig.9].[7] These were written between the end of 1923 and early 1925. They fill an important gap as, hitherto, Macdonald's has been the missing voice from France. None of her replies to Mackintosh's extended *Chronycle* survive. Now we have a suggestion of her gentle humour, her appreciation of the detail of her surroundings, and also a sense of her, and doubtless their, positive outlook. 'We like life here so much and Toshie is as happy as a sandboy – tremendously interested in his painting and, of course, doing some remarkable work.'[8]

The three letters add valuable insights to our understanding of the couple's first year in France. They establish that their first base was Amélie-les-Bains, where they stayed for at least two months from late 1923. By spring 1924 they were considering trying out Collioure, which they had visited and found delightful. The difficulty was in finding suitable accommodation: 'It is only a fishing village and it will be difficult to find accommodation – and there is no hotel – but I expect we shall manage somehow.'[9] It now seems likely that the decision to be based in the nearby working port of Port Vendres, rather than the more picturesque Collioure, was less of a deliberate choice to protect their privacy, as has previously been thought, and more a pragmatic decision in order to secure suitable catered lodgings. Macdonald's frequent comments about hotel costs show how carefully they had to watch their budget. It is clear that there was initial uncertainty about how long they would stay, and, therefore, they retained their rented studios in London 'till we return + decide what it is best to do –'[10] Over that first year, though, they clearly fell in love with the Roussillon. After a brief visit to London in late 1924 she wrote with obvious pleasure, 'We came on here – to this lovely rose-colored land + we were glad to be back again in its warmth + sun.'[11] In the autumn of 1924 the couple had travelled back to London, to re-let their London studios, returning to France in November. En route they visited their friend and a former client of Mackintosh's, the Scottish painter R. Macaulay Stevenson at Montreuil-sur-Mer, a place they did not care for. 'It is very like Winchelsea – a little hill town in a marshy plain + it was much too damp for our taste.'[12] They subsequently stopped in Paris, to view the Autumn Salon exhibition, before heading south to Amélie and then Ille-sur-Têt where they planned to stay until May 1925.

Margaret Macdonald's first letter to Jessie Newbery sets out that the couple had rented two studios in Amélie:

> *We have taken this tiny house, it has just two rooms – one on top of the other (I think it must have been the old Toll house), for studios, and we are living at the little hotel just across the bridge, at one end of which this house stands. The hotel is simple but beautifully clean and the cooking amazing. It is very cheap so that suits us …*[13]

Their plan must have been to re-establish the successful arrangement they had had in London, of rented lodgings and individual

LEFT TO RIGHT

Fig.2 | E.O. Hoppé
*Charles Rennie Mackintosh c.*1920
Hunterian Art Gallery, University of Glasgow

Fig.3 | *Margaret Macdonald Mackintosh c.*1929, passport photograph
Hunterian Art Gallery, University of Glasgow

Fig.4 | Glasgow School of Art
Mark Fiennes

Fig.5 | The Hill House
The National Trust for Scotland

Fig.6 | Ladies Luncheon Room, Miss Cranston's Tea Rooms, Ingram Street, Glasgow
Glasgow Museums: Kelvingrove Art Gallery and Museum

studios. Hitherto it has been assumed that Macdonald ceased all creative work before the move abroad. None the less, no work by her from France is known, and at some point the studios were given up, probably for financial reasons. For the first time in his long career, Mackintosh would have been without a dedicated workspace. Instead, his studio was the great outdoors.

The narrative is picked up two years later, in May and June 1927, in the pages of *The Chronycle*. These letters provide our fullest account of the Mackintoshes' lives in France. On the basis of Mackintosh's descriptions of his daily activities, the couple led a modest life in Port Vendres, walking and reading, observing the activity in the busy harbour, enjoying the local fish, cherries and wine. Mackintosh made gentle efforts to learn to speak French. Their lives were rooted in their own company, and given a discipline by Mackintosh's painting.

The Chronycle also records Mackintosh's blistered and swollen tongue, the first indication of the terminal cancer which was to force the couple back to London at the end of 1927. Mackintosh died there in December of the following year. The four years after his death were restless and lonely ones for Margaret Macdonald, and she was troubled by ill health. She strove to place the watercolours with galleries in London, and to have them published. Most, however, remained in her Chelsea studio or in store with a London framer until her death in early 1933. The French watercolours were not seen publicly as a group until the *Mackintosh Memorial Exhibition* held in Glasgow later that year [fig.1]. Nearly thirty were on display, scattered between architectural drawings, metalwork, flower drawings and photographs. They were a revelation to the Glasgow audience, who had little knowledge of Mackintosh's career after his departure for Walberswick. One thoughtful critic for the *Glasgow Evening Citizen* concluded:

> *It is not often that an architect is also master of the art of landscape painting. In the virile and eminently decorative landscapes of Mackintosh we have another revelation of his power and consummate artistry ... Mackintosh seizes with unerring instinct upon the essential forms in natural structure and, with extraordinary strength of drawing and fearless use of pure colour-washes, gives us a statement which at once records facts truthfully and creates a beauty which is entirely personal. Surely, directly, without fumbling, he interprets the patterns he finds in Nature, in buildings and in the loveliness of things that grow.*

THE FRENCH WATERCOLOURS

From the outset of his career, Mackintosh had painted and maintained close friendships with artists. Artistry was a central thread in his life and work. At different points, painting provided the opportunity for creative experimentation, for relaxation and recuperation, and for a new career, culminating in the French watercolours. The French paintings should, therefore, not be seen as a self-contained period in Mackintosh's career, a resilient response to changed personal circumstances. Rather, they form another phase in his career as a painter and artistically are an almost inevitable outcome of preoccupations which can be traced back to his student days. They present a merging of his deep-rooted interest in painting, nature and buildings, founded on drawing skills honed in the art school studio and the architect's office.

By 1924, Mackintosh had had forty years experience of architecture, starting as an apprentice with John Hutchison, Glasgow, in 1884, and subsequently working with Honeyman & Keppie, Glasgow from 1889, initially as draughtsman. The preparation of plans and elevations as a junior in the office required precision of technique and, doubtless, discipline of temperament. There would be much to do in what was one of the busier practices in the city. Even once a partner, from 1901, Mackintosh retained a hand's-on role in the draughtsmanship.[14] Such work was founded on the schematic representation of three-dimensional form in two dimensions. Parallels can be seen between Mackintosh's professional elevation drawings and the significant number of French watercolours that include frontal views of buildings and townscapes.

Observing, analysing and recording buildings and their component parts *in situ* had been an integral part of Mackintosh's experience as a young student. In common with other apprentice architects, Mackintosh would escape from the office to the open air and the study of historic architecture. He spoke passionately of being impelled by the 'irresistible attraction ... not only under the balmy influences of summer, but along muddy roads and snowy path, and with glowing heart but shivering hand to sketch the humble cottage the more pretentious mansion or the mutilated though venerable castle ...'[15] Through the 1890s travels in Scotland were principally located in the central belt, taking in Ayrshire, Stirling, Linlithgow, Fife, and elsewhere, with occasionally longer trips further afield to Morayshire, Bute and Arran. These were variously in connection with work in the practice, for example, Honeyman's restoration of Glasgow Cathedral (1890–1) and St Michael's Church, Linlithgow (1894–6); the outings of the Glasgow Architectural Association; or as part of the Glasgow School of Art Club's annual summer sketching assignments. In the 1890s, regular tours were made in England, to Hampshire, Dorset, Somerset, Norfolk and Devon. And in 1891, Mackintosh had undertaken an eight-week sketching tour of Italy, taking in Paris, Brussels and Antwerp on the return journey.

The sketchbooks are filled with 'bits', 'notes', 'jottings' – shorthand details gathered together like cuttings in a succession of scrapbooks. What they reveal is Mackintosh's drawing technique away from the office drawing board. We see a hand that is economic, expressive, fluent, which expresses form through outline, as in the sketch of Maybole Castle [fig.10]. We see an eye that is interested in profile, frequently in elements such as a cupola or tower, one that is interested in window and door openings, and in decorative carving, ironwork and inscriptions. Just occasionally we see a more romantic eye, which captured the striking silhouette of Stirling Castle on its dramatic volcanic rock, touched by the setting sun [fig.11]

Mackintosh continued to sketch for the next twenty-five years; his last recorded drawing is a delightful study of a small house in Walberswick, dated 1914. By that time, many of the drawings had become more complex. Their initial role had been to provide inspiration, source material and self-definition for an eager and as yet untried architect. By the early 1900s circumstances were different. Mackintosh was successful, busy and married. Sketching, however, was not abandoned. It evolved into considered and

LEFT TO RIGHT

Fig.7 | Rudolph Ihlee
Fort Precincts, Collioure 1927
Hunterian Art Gallery, University of Glasgow

Fig.8 | Thornton Oakley *The Village of Palalda*
From Amy Oakley, *The Hill-Towns of the Pyrénées*,
The Century Co., New York 1923

Fig.9 | *Jessie Newbery* c.1930
Glasgow School of Art

Fig.10 | C.R. Mackintosh
Maybole Castle, Ayrshire 1895
Hunterian Art Gallery, University of Glasgow

Fig.11 | C.R. Mackintosh
Stirling Castle at Sunset
National Library of Ireland

Fig.12 | C.R. Mackintosh
Castle, Holy Island 1901
Hunterian Art Gallery, University of Glasgow

sophisticated compositions whose core focus remained that of capturing, with pencil and the occasional touch of watercolour, elements of the local architecture, whether a well in Cintra, Portugal, in 1908, or a picturesque street in Chiddingstone, Kent, in 1910.

These years of sketching honed Mackintosh's skills of observation and close analysis, refined his drawing technique and accustomed him to working *en plein air*, with the minimum of equipment. Such skills underpinned the watercolours in France, where the initial drawing on the paper, subsequently erased, must have closely resembled the outline skeletons of drawings such as those of Holy Island [fig.12]. The elevations of Palalda and Bouleternère, punctuated by their many window openings, can be viewed as larger versions of the palaces Mackintosh had sketched in Italy – [see plates 1 & 2].

No sketchbooks from London or from France survive. And yet there was much, in France at least, that in earlier days would have made him reach eagerly for his pencil, such as the impressive local ironwork, which adorned the churches and castles that the couple visited, and the medieval fragments which were such a feature of Ille-sur-Têt. We know that the couple travelled extensively, seeking out remote early churches. By 1925 they had visited Elne, Arles-sur-Tech, Prats-de-Mollo, Montalba, Montbolo, Marins, Jujols, Canavels, Palalda and others.[16] It may simply be that such sketchbooks have not survived; or it may be that the new lifestyle in France, free of other commitments, meant that his focus shifted from sketches, done in an afternoon, to watercolour compositions developed over several weeks.

Parallels with the French paintings can be found with another form of architectural drawing. As early as the mid-1890s, Mackintosh had been composing buildings and landscape settings in showpiece perspective drawings. These were important public images for reproduction in the architectural press and for exhibition, and therefore important both for the architectural practice and the individual draughtsman. Mackintosh used the established formula of setting the building at three-quarters angle, but added a spacious foreground and heavily worked sky. The whole was distinguished by his extravagant line drawing and decorative hatching, which left areas of the paper untouched to form the substance of the composition. Through such means an ordinary warehouse or a university building acquired an eye-catching glamour [fig.13]. Early on Mackintosh had recognised the value of manipulated viewpoints – of space around the subject and areas of detail and void – to dramatise the ordinary. Similar compositional techniques re-emerge in the French watercolours. Compare, for example, the perspective of Queen Margaret College with the composition of the farm building in *Blanc Ontoine* [plate 6] or the houses in *A Southern Town* [plate 12]. Or consider its decorative use of selected shrubs and paths with the composition of *The Fort* [plate 25]. Both the perspective drawings and the French watercolours present controlled manipulations of their subjects: they are about design. Despite his lively interest in the daily happenings of Port Vendres, and his eagerness to share these by letter with his wife, the activity of human life is excised from his compositions, and the turbulence of nature excluded.

The appearance of developed watercolour compositions of

Fig.13 | C.R. Mackintosh
Queen Margaret's Medical College, University of Glasgow – perspective 1895
Private collection

Fig.14 | C.R. Mackintosh
Glasgow Cathedral at Sunset 1890
Hunterian Art Gallery, University of Glasgow

buildings or landscape before the move to London is rare, with the exception of a small group of youthful watercolours from the 1890s. The first of these is *Glasgow Cathedral at Sunset*, dating from 1890 [fig.14]. The lowering medieval cathedral was the landmark building near Mackintosh's family home. It would have been familiar to him too from the interests of his employer, John Honeyman, who was charged with its restoration in the early 1890s; Mackintosh himself had sketched details of it in the late 1880s. The watercolour shows the building silhouetted against an evening sky shot with colour. The foreground is generalised. *The Lido* was an experimental painting possibly executed on his tour of Italy in 1891, which concluded in the north of Italy in Venice and Milan [fig.15]. Sketches of gondolas are contained in the notebooks recording his tour. The composition, subject matter, technique, and even the framing are indebted to James McNeill Whistler. This more allusive approach to subject matter, where form is suggested through wash and brushwork, was not repeated by Mackintosh. *Porlock Weir* is an intriguing work, normally dated to the mid-1890s when Mackintosh made a series of sketching trips to England [fig.16]. This conventional composition of sun-drenched cottages in Somerset could be the work of other artists, yet an inscription on the back secures its authorship.Often omitted from discussion of Mackintosh's painting, it is intriguing to see him working on this scale and to this level of finish at such an early date. Of this early group, *Wareham*, probably made on his 1895 trip to Dorset, is the most telling. This dramatic watercolour initially engages through its vibrant colour palette. The work is a skilfully organised composition. Nearly two thirds of the composition is a flat grey sky, punctuated by the tower of Wareham church and a solitary tree. The frontages of the village houses form a band across the middle ground, one white elevation stands out, and the band is cut across by the shallow diagonals of the bridge and fence. The foreground is sketched in with green wash. Similar 'banding' was to become a central element of the French watercolours in, for example, *The Church of La Llagonne* [plate 35] or *Port Vendres* [plate 14].

Mackintosh does not appear to have returned to this subject matter or to the format of developed watercolour compositions during the remaining Glasgow years, doubtless due to demands elsewhere in his career. Rather, he expressed his interest in nature in his design work. 'Real' nature was brought into his interiors, but manipulated and made to appear designed, as in the floral arrangements in his home at 120 Mains Street, Glasgow. Long stems of *Clematis montana* were twisted and turned to form striking ball shapes, which resemble 'natural' barbed wire. The forms of trees and plant growth inspired some of his most iconic furniture and decorative schemes, while the rose imbued the decoration of the principal bedroom at The Hill House and the room setting designed with Margaret Macdonald for the *International Exhibition of Modern Decorative Art*, Turin, in 1902. And he continued with the botanical drawings that had filled many pages of his sketchbooks.

Some thirty pencil studies of plants are contained in the sketchbooks from his travels in Scotland and England. Like his architectural studies they explore outline and detail, occasionally presenting elements alongside the main plant as plans and elevations, much like his analyses of campanile or the profiles of

Fig.15 | C.R. Mackintosh *The Lido* c.1891
Hunterian Art Gallery, University of Glasgow

Fig.16 | C.R. Mackintosh *Porlock Weir* mid-1890s
Hunterian Art Gallery, University of Glasgow

cornices and jambs. These works too, became more developed, and culminated in the watercolours of flowers painted in Walberswick. This botanical subject matter was richly exploited during the couple's subsequent years in London, from 1915 to 1923, both for progressive textile designs, and for sophisticated and beautifully coloured still-life compositions.

The move to Walberswick was intended to provide an opportunity for rest and to recover from his failure to set up an independent practice in Glasgow. In the absence of design work, Mackintosh rediscovered landscape painting, encouraged by his painter companions, Francis Newbery, the Glasgow Boy painter E.A. Walton (1860–1922), and the English landscape artist, Bertram Priestman (1868–1921). Three watercolours are known: *Venetian Palace, Blackshore-on-the-Blyth*, *A Palace of Timber* and *Walberswick* [figs.18–20]. The first two, of modest riverside netting warehouses, must have evoked for Mackintosh the faded grandeur of Venice's grand palazzi. All three show the emerging preoccupations that were to dominate the French watercolours: water, reflections, buildings, harbours and landscape. The palette of these works is more subdued and the medium more broadly handled than in the later, meticulous French paintings.

It was again in the company of close artist friends that Mackintosh once more painted on this scale, during a holiday in Dorset with the artist and teacher, Randolph Schwabe, and his family. Two landscapes survive, both probably from 1920: *The Village, Worth Matravers* and *The Downs, Worth Matravers* [figs.21 & 22]. *The Village* shows Worth's picturesque cottages nestled on a gently sloping hillside, in a seemingly informal arrangement comparable to *Slate Roofs* [plate 29]. *The Downs* takes a broader view, from a high vantage point looking out to the sea. Its composition is anchored by the great central telegraph pole. Mackintosh's main interest is the curves and sweeps of the landscape, a theme taken up in his studies of French mountain landscape [plates 36–8].

Two sketches related to *The Village* survive, showing studies of the houses in the centre and to the right of the composition, and revealing the careful preparation which underpinned the composition [figs. 23 & 24]. These are intriguing works, which are either a rare survival or a one-off instance. They are the only known examples of sketches related to a developed watercolour composition. These drawings are not on pages from a sketchbook, but are on the back of sheets of notepaper headed with Mackintosh's London address. He has used a softer pencil and a broader stroke than appear in the known sketchbooks. The draughtsmanship, if not the pencil, suggests they are by Mackintosh and the probability is that they are sketches made *in situ*, rather than the studio, most likely to help work in progress. No such sketches are known in France. The compositions there were shaped during periods of close study in front of the subject, some of which are recorded in *The Chronycle*, 'I went out to see my new view of Fort Moresque and just as well – I must know all about it before I begin and I think that must be very soon now.' (15 May, 3.3) He returned for another look a few days later. (18 May, 5.2)

The Chronycle and the surviving watercolours provide valuable insight into Mackintosh's working practice in France.[17] He used the minimum of equipment: a prepared paper-mounted millboard of a size that was easy to carry, usually around 40 × 40 centimetres,

LEFT TO RIGHT

Fig.17 | C.R. Mackintosh
Wareham 1895
Hida Takayama Museum, Japan

Fig.18 | C.R. Mackintosh
A Palace of Timber c.1914
Work destroyed

Fig.19 | C.R. Mackintosh
Venetian Palace, Blackshore-on-the-Blyth 1914
Hunterian Art Gallery, University of Glasgow

Fig.20 | C.R. Mackintosh
Walberswick 1914
Private collection

lead tubes of watercolour paint, an enamelled sketcher's palette, mixing dish, rubber, ruler, brushes, pocket knife, water container, and a brush-washing cup. He does not appear to have used an umbrella, easel or stool. Unencumbered he could scramble to the best locations on rocks or hillsides from which to secure his preferred vantage points. In Port Vendres and Collioure, at least, that also involved shelter from the fierce tramontane wind, which regularly threatened his board and disrupted his plans for painting.

It was perfect this morning at 6 o'clock at 7 o'clock and at 8 o'clock when I started out, but when I got to my place it began to blow and the blow increased until it was half a gale – it took me half the morning to find a sheltered place ... The wind seemed to fall during lunch time so I tried again on the 'autre coté' but it was no use – I could not hold my card-board steady enough to draw properly. (13 May, 2.2)

A clear routine was established of painting from early in the morning till lunchtime, occasionally going out to work in the afternoon. It is conspicuous that the majority of his subjects are within a short walking distance of their accommodation, whether in Amélie, Ille-sur-Têt or Port Vendres; Mackintosh needed to be able to return to enjoy lunch with his wife.

The painting best documented in *The Chronycle* is *The Rock* [plate 28] though Mackintosh does refer to considering starting a larger version of the subject.[18] In his opening letter on 12 May, he advises, 'The day has been perfect, bright sun and not a breath of wind so I had a good mornings work and the picture of the ROCK goes well'. Four days later, further progress has been made: 'All my little village is painted and now I dread to contemplate I have to commence my big Rock perhaps it will come out all right – but I seem to work very slowly'. (16 May, 4.4) He was more confident a week later: 'This morning has been superb – sun and no wind, I have now broken the back of the rock and it will now do what I want it to do – so if this no wind continues it should be finished tomorrow'. (24 May, 6.4) His ambition was not quite fulfilled as his letter the next day records: 'Had a lovely morning – absolutely superb. Working all morning at the Rock not yet finished but getting on.' (25 May, 7.2) It was still not finished by 3 June: 'This morning was perfectly lovely and I got 4 hours work at the Rock – I want just one perfectly still morning – no wind – no waves – not a ripple then I can finish the reflection of the Rock and that will mean another picture put away.' (3 June, 11.1) Nor was it finished by 11 June: 'I had a long and perfect morning at my "ROCK" but it is not yet finished or signed – each time I work at it it developes but another morning like this should see it finished and I shall make a special effort to remember a place for the signature.' (11 June, 15.1–2) Finally success is recorded on 13 June: 'My "ROCK" is finished all but the signature.' (13 June, 16.1)

This account hints at Mackintosh's considered rate of progress – some seven sessions of several hours each are recorded here, working on a composition which had already been started before Macdonald's departure. Mackintosh acknowledged his lack of speed. 'I go very slow because I have still so many problems to solve'. (21 June, 21A) Progress was dependent on calm, bright days, which that summer proved elusive. The letters also show that work was completed in stages, the background view of Port Vendres being completed before the central subject of the rock itself was tackled. It seems to have been a common occurrence for him to

forget to sign his works. Elsewhere in *The Chronycle* he advises Macdonald to sign the works she had with her in London, and in the final weeks of his life, he reputedly signed *La Rue du Soleil* [plate 16] and *The Little Bay* [plate 17] from his hospital bed.

While the watercolours are substantially based on Mackintosh's experience and concerns as an architect and designer, other relationships can be identified. Parallels can be made with the highly disciplined compositions, flattened perspective, unmodulated colour and decorative outline of Japanese woodblock prints, of which Mackintosh owned examples. The architectural subject matter of Whistler's prints, in particular his Venice etchings, with their interest in façades, window and door openings, rooflines, and reflections, must have delighted Mackintosh [fig.25]. His Walberswick *Venetian Palace* may be as much a tribute to Whistler as to Venice. The stylisations and bold colours of the London graphic designs for Bassett-Lowke Ltd [fig.37] were closely akin to contemporary, progressive Vorticist ideas, and were developed, for example, in the handling of the rock formations in *Fort Mailly* [plate 26] and *The Rock* [plate 28]. More tantalising, and more speculative, is any secure relationship with Cubism. Mackintosh would have encountered the work of Cézanne and the Cubists at the very least on the walls of the International Society exhibitions in London, where he himself exhibited between 1915 and 1917. Parallels can be made with their concerns with fracturing form and setting up complex spatial games. A playfulness with form can be seen as early as the sketches of Holy Island or Cintra, in the early 1900s, in which outline drawings of different elements are overlaid to create two-dimensional collages.

Mackintosh was ambitious for his painting. He strove for improvement: 'I find that each of my drawings has something in them but none of them have everything. This must be remedied.' (28 May, 8.5) 'I am trying for something else.' (1 June, 10.1) 'You know that even in the brightest sunshine my pictures are still very sombre – at least that is what I feel about them and I want to get more and more light.' (15 June, 17.1) A heightening of the colour palette is clearly apparent between early farmhouse watercolours, such as *Blanc Ontoine*, and later Port Vendres views such as *The Little Bay*. Equally a progression towards more complex manipulations of viewpoints and more meticulous draughtsmanship and application of the watercolour medium, is evident if one compares the undoubtedly early *The Road through the Rocks* [plate 24] with *The Fort* [plate 25]. There is also a more sophisticated handling of form, culminating in the highly disciplined patterns created from shadows and ripples in *The Little Bay* and the deconstruction of form when reflected in an eddying sea in *La Rue du Soleil*. *La Rue du Soleil* typifies the contrasts which so appealed to Mackintosh: here between object and reflection, land and sea, still and moving; and elsewhere between man-made and natural architecture, or wild and cultivated land. Occasionally a more modest detail became the focus of attention, such as the splendid cockerel, silhouetted in the doorway of *A Southern Farm* [plate 9], or the bollard and its shadow, in the foreground of *The Little Bay*, which together are given the dignity of a still-life centrepiece. The idea of Mackintosh's wit should not be overlooked. Alan Crawford drew attention to the conceit of a playful, watchful eye motif, which is incorporated into the metalwork detailing of a

Mackintosh wardrobe.[19] One can perhaps see in *Palalda, Pyrénées-Orientales* [plate 1] a similar trick, where the lone white building peers out from the centre. Yet the remarkable achievement is that, although the subjects have been filtered through Mackintosh's creative mind, they remain topographically accurate and readily identifiable.

Mackintosh was also eager for commercial and critical success. 'I dont think you can speak of my work untill *[sic]* you see it exposed side by side with others in some show ... it must take its place and hold its own in any company'. (1 June, 10.2) But such success did not happen in his lifetime. Only a few of the water-colours are known to have been exhibited and only two sold before his early death in 1928. The first substantial showing was not until 1933 when thirty of the French paintings were included in the *Mackintosh Memorial Exhibition*, Glasgow. Thereafter the works were not seen as a significant group until the landmark centenary exhibition of 1968, in Edinburgh. The situation is markedly different today and Mackintosh's paintings are held in major print rooms around the world. As recently as 2004, the Art Institute of Chicago acquired *Collioure* [plate 11]. And in Port Vendres initiatives are underway to provide permanent markers to the quiet, productive years the Mackintoshes spent in France.

BELOW LEFT TO RIGHT

Fig.21 | C.R. Mackintosh *The Village, Worth Matravers* *c.*1920
Glasgow School of Art

Fig.22 | C.R. Mackintosh *The Downs, Worth Matravers* *c.*1920
Glasgow School of Art

Fig.23 | C.R. Mackintosh *Worth Matravers* *c.*1920
Hunterian Art Gallery, University of Glasgow

Fig.24 | C.R. Mackintosh *Worth Matravers* *c.*1920
Hunterian Art Gallery, University of Glasgow

RIGHT

Fig.25 | J. M. Whistler *The Palaces* 1879
Hunterian Art Gallery, University of Glasgow

C. R. Mackintosh *Ships* c.1922
Private collection

CHARLES RENNIE MACKINTOSH: A PAINTER AMONGST PAINTERS

PHILIP LONG

When Mackintosh moved abroad in 1923, he began a period in his life and working practice which, in comparison with all the phases of his earlier career, can be characterised by its isolation. In France he produced a body of work that was required to satisfy nothing more than his critical temperament and a wish that his efforts might culminate in an exhibition. This is in marked contrast to the years for which he remains best known, the decade or so around 1900, when his work and his professional reputation were shaped in a more public way: through his relationship with clients, his critical reception, and his contact with progressive artists across Europe.

For Mackintosh, however, this vital period was short, and from around 1910 the story of his career is traditionally seen as one of decline. Fourteen years separate the completion of his final major building project (the second phase of the Glasgow School of Art, finished in 1909) and his departure for France. A range of circumstances contributed to Mackintosh's difficulties during this time, not least changing fashions in architecture and the paralysing effects of the First World War. Although Mackintosh remained active as a designer and painter, the succession of unrealised architectural projects exacerbates a perception that his late watercolours are remote and detached in style from his earlier work. There was virtually no public awareness of the paintings he produced in France until their inclusion in the *Mackintosh Memorial Exhibition* held in 1933, a fact that contributes to a romantic interpretation of Mackintosh's later circumstances. The paintings themselves, however, are made with a conviction and have a coherence which emphasises their importance to Mackintosh as a new phase in his work and, for him, the circumstances of their making must have been liberating.

Mackintosh's French paintings are not made with the radical approach to art and design that characterises his more startling early work. In turning full-time to painting, it is fascinating to think that Mackintosh might have developed as fresh an artistic language as he had in his designs from the 1890s onwards, which as a young man had surprised his contemporaries and brought him attention from across Europe. The fact that his late paintings were not overtly avant-garde should not be interpreted as a consequence of a failing imagination. Rather, his French watercolours can be seen as a natural, fully orchestrated development of the sketches of buildings and landscapes he first made while a student, a development which is traced through the introductory works in this exhibition and more fully in the preceding essay. Here, it is important to emphasise that from the outset of his career Mackintosh produced sketches of buildings and landscapes and in some of the most interesting of these explored the interweaving of the man-made and the natural, as he would in his French works thirty-five years later. In tune with Arts and Crafts ideals and those of Fra Newbery, the director of the Glasgow School of Art who fostered Mackintosh's talent, Mackintosh always viewed himself as an artist, and artistic values constantly underpinned his work as an architect and designer. His sketches played a crucial part in the development of his architectural vocabulary; they can be described as the germ from which his innovative designs grew. Painting itself remained important for him throughout his career and if his late works are considered in a broader artistic context, we find that not only are they in tune with British painting of the time, but they also show Mackintosh's wider knowledge of recent developments in European art.

Mackintosh's early sketches and watercolours, which were made in Scotland and while on a travelling scholarship to Italy in 1891, are relatively straightforward architectural studies, completed to varying degrees of finish and scale. From 1892 his interests diversified as he began to use the medium of watercolour to develop a series of mystical, otherworldly paintings, populated by strange forms and figures of arcane symbolism. Together with his friend and architectural associate Herbert McNair and the sisters Frances and Margaret Macdonald, Mackintosh was a protagonist in the development of what has become known as the Glasgow Style, distinguishing it in locale from its symbolist counterparts across Europe. At the same time, Mackintosh's professional career as an architect was developing within the firm of Honeyman & Keppie and his output of independent artworks slowed as his attention turned to expressing his vision through commissioned design. What seems clear, however, is that the sketches and watercolours produced during the early part of his career established a pattern in his work that was of importance not only to the development of his architecture, but which also paved the way for the watercolours he would eventually produce in France.

From 1894, Mackintosh began to go on sketching trips around England, mostly to rural areas such as the Cotswolds, Hampshire, Somerset and Dorset. The sketchbooks he filled fed his architectural imagination, but he also completed more finished watercolours. His view of *Wareham* [see fig.17], a Dorset village he visited in 1895, has a strong horizontal emphasis, the empty foreground and sky separated by a row of close-planned buildings of a regular height broken by the rise of the church tower and an adjacent tree. This carefully structured approach to composition, where perspective is suppressed in favour of a composition built in strata from bottom to top, already prefigures many of the French paintings, and in particular *Bouleternère* [plate 2], where the interlocking buildings and roofs rise up to a centrally placed church situated above the village skyline. In that particular work Mackintosh brought together two separate views of the village, aligning one above the other to create a vertically inclined composition (see p.34). The few landscapes Mackintosh completed in the 1890s also share similarities with the artist's contemporaneous symbolist paintings. In *Wareham* the trees, shown looming in front of the village, are painted in a thin watercolour technique akin to the rounded and flower-like forms in *The Tree of Influence* [fig.26], one of Mackintosh's most important symbolist paintings of the period. In both works, and identifiable throughout Mackintosh's oeuvre, there is a distinction between structural and biomorphic forms. Mackintosh's interest in the relationship between the built and the natural environment is already evident in such early works as *Wareham*, but becomes obvious in later drawings of houses in Sussex and Kent, made in 1909 [fig.27], where the artist combines natural growth and constructed form with a fascination that results in highly imaginative compositions, rich in pattern and pulsating with life.

In France Mackintosh found a landscape of a different character from that of the southern counties of England. The regularity of building type and huddled planning of the inland towns and hilltop villages of the Roussillon make up, to this day, an architectural landscape where individual buildings appear to be interconnected. Compositions such as *Palalda, Pyrénées-Orientales* [plate 1] highlight this. Mackintosh excludes the surrounding landscape, restricting his visual field to show the hillside village as a man-made edifice rising from the river bed. This approach is reminiscent of the view expressed by the Viennese artist Gustav Klimt, that he had painted some of his landscapes with the aid of a telescope, and in other cases had defined his composition by using a viewfinder, 'a (square) hole cut in the lid of a cardboard box'.[1] Klimt was first president of the Vienna Secession (the name given to the group of progressive artists who, in 1897, broke away from the Viennese establishment), and it has been suggested that he was deeply impressed by the Mackintoshes' gesso panels in the Scottish room shown at the Secession exhibition in 1900, to the extent that they influenced the format of his 1902 *Beethoven Frieze*.[2] Klimt is now as well known for his landscape paintings as he is for his more overtly symbolist works, executing these during periods of relaxation and escapism in the country. As Mackintosh began to

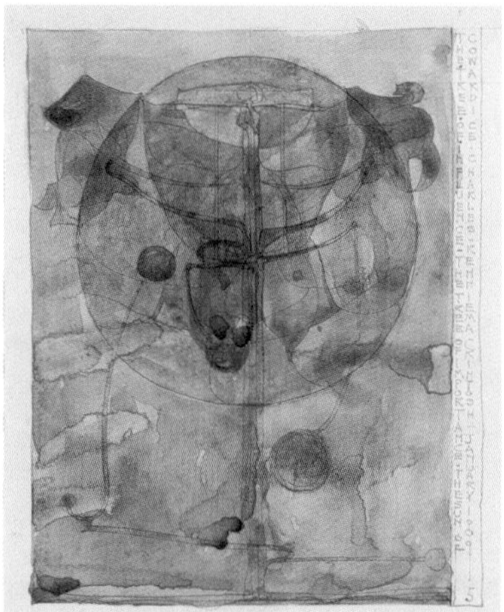

Fig.26 | C.R. Mackintosh *The Tree of Influence* 1895
Glasgow School of Art

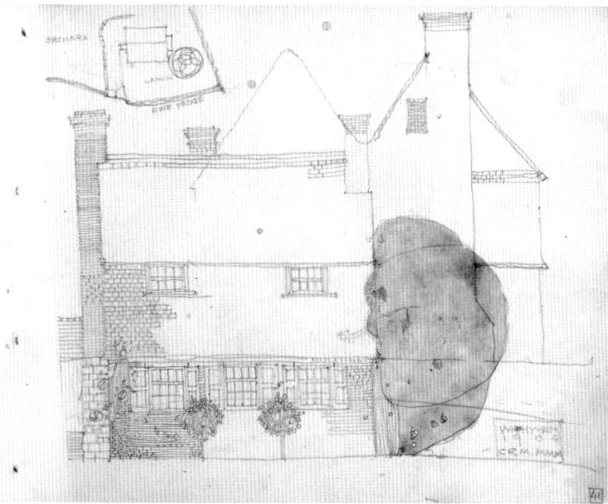

Fig.27 | C.R. Mackintosh *House at Withyham, Sussex* 1909
Hunterian Art Gallery, University of Glasgow

Fig.28 | Gustav Klimt *Malcesine on Lake Garda* 1913
Work destroyed

paint full time, he may in turn have looked to Klimt, whose works, such as *Malcesine on Lake Garda* from 1913 [fig.28], share not only a similar interest in picturesque subject matter, but also the square format and high horizon (sometimes excluded altogether) that we see in a number of Mackintosh's French paintings. Egon Schiele too, who worked under the influence of Klimt, produced townscapes in a similar manner in the early 1910s, favouring a bird's-eye view and depicting settlements as if they were constructed from building blocks [fig.29].

The French landscape motifs Mackintosh was naturally drawn to were typically rocky outcrops, integrated with cultivated landscape terraces, which give the steep hillsides a geometric, man-made structure. For Mackintosh this provided a natural pattern, which he incorporated in his compositions, as he had done with the striations in the land in his 1920 painting, *The Downs, Worth Matravers* [see fig.22]. Mackintosh gave prominent attention to such features, the effect of which shows his interest in the abstract potential of his subject matter. This is particularly clear in works such as *Port Vendres, La Ville* [plate 15], where the detailed attention paid to the steeply rising land beyond the town adds to the complexity of the composition's perspective. Indeed, in France, with the exception of works such as *A Southern Port* [plate 13], which uses a more traditional perspective of gradual recession to a distant point (and which has consequently been dated from the beginning of his time spent there), Mackintosh appears to have deliberately chosen subjects where land and buildings rose up before him, in a sense presenting him with compositions face-on. His interest in the forms of Japanese architecture is well known, and he would have been aware of the perspective techniques in Japanese landscape paintings and prints, where rising features are ranged alternately one above the other. A variation of such an approach can be discerned in examples of Mackintosh's vertically composed sketches, where he pays attention to particular details as they appear over the façade of a building, or within plants. In his buildings, this is no better expressed than in the towering façade of the library wing of Glasgow School Art, where the fenestration becomes increasingly elaborate as it rises through the courses of the elevation [fig.30].

Mackintosh's French paintings are densely worked. He uses line, pattern and colour to map out and distinguish features, which are treated in a non-hierarchical way regardless of their relative distance. Areas of flat colour representing sky in the very upper reaches relieve the sheer amount of detail within his compositions. Isolated buildings are more plainly depicted, in particular, the simple, flat elevations of Fort Mailly at Port Vendres [plate 26]. Mackintosh used this technique in his landscape paintings created in the formative years of his career, when he would have been conscious of the advances made by the Glasgow School painters. Motifs in works such as E.A. Walton's *Helensburgh* (shown at the Royal Scottish Society of Watercolours in 1886 [fig.31]), for example, the strong emphasis on the horizontal and the flat expanse of the foreground, are used as the compositional base for works such as *Porlock Weir* and *Wareham* [see figs.16 & 17] and other works. While Mackintosh's extraordinary symbolist paintings of the same period seem removed from the realist, rural subject matter favoured by the Glasgow Boys (as the Glasgow School also became

Fig.29 | Egon Schiele
The Small Town II 1912/13
The Leopold Collection, Vienna

Fig.30 | C.R. Mackintosh
Glasgow School of Art, the West Wing
Glasgow School of Art

Fig.31 | E.A. Walton
Helensburgh 1886
Hunterian Art Gallery, University of Glasgow

known), connections can be made between this aspect of Mackintosh's art and the most progressive works of that group. By the late 1880s Arthur Melville's brilliant, free watercolour technique had inspired many Scottish artists in the use of that medium. *The Tree of Influence* may represent a quite different, otherworldly view from Melville's watercolour of 1893, *Autumn – Loch Lomond* [fig.32], but Mackintosh's leap beyond Melville's naturalism is interesting in the context of recent developments in the work of two other Glasgow Boys, George Henry and E.A. Hornel (the latter a close friend of Mackintosh's employer, John Keppie). By about 1890 and on occasion working collaboratively, they had developed a new phase in their art which is strongly symbolic in content (commonly featuring mythical or sprite-like figures shown intertwined with nature), and so linked directly with the art of Mackintosh, McNair and the Macdonald sisters. A friend and contemporary of Mackintosh's at Glasgow School of Art was another of the Glasgow Boys, David Gauld, whose *St Agnes* [fig.33] of 1889 anticipates the elongated symbolist figures of Mackintosh and his associates' graphic style of the mid-1890s. *St Agnes* was shown along with other works by the Glasgow School at the Munich International Exhibition of 1890, where their innovative painting contributed to the artistic discord that led to the formation of the Munich Secession in 1893. A stylistic analysis of Gauld's *St Agnes*, in particular, his treatment of the landscape and distant village, suggests Mackintosh may have returned to a memory of this work as he formulated his French paintings. This may also have been the case with George Henry's *A Galloway Landscape* [fig.34], also painted in 1889 and identified as one of the most innovative Glasgow School paintings of the period. Henry's work shows a rural hillside, and while it has many of the characteristics of the Glasgow School's art of that date – in particular a raking landscape bounded by a high horizon, motifs evident in Mackintosh's French paintings – Henry's sinuous, curving river-form recurs in a number of Mackintosh's inland French subjects. Mackintosh's depiction of the road that rises up and branches across *Mont Alba* [plate 5] – painted high up in the deep gorge at Montalba d'Amélie (to the south of Amélie-les-Bains) – provides that work with the same decorative effect achieved by Henry, and we find this repeated in the serpentine track climbing through the unknown location of *A Hill Town in Southern France* [plate 4].

As Mackintosh turned full time to painting in the 1920s, such links with the 1890s may have seemed remote, and if a connection is to be made with the art of the Glasgow School, then a work such as Arthur Melville's *A Sapphire Sea* [fig.35], painted on the Spanish coast in 1892, more obviously shares Mackintosh's interest in the reductive effect of strong light on water and buildings. However, Mackintosh's geometrical, angular design and his use of repeating motifs (done with great contrasting effect in the *The Little Bay, Port Vendres* [plate 17], with its stylised curving waves and zigzag balustrade shadows), makes clear that his French painting is the product of a more modern artistic sensibility, and succeeds the dynamism of his wartime textile designs [fig.37] and the work at Derngate, the Northampton home of W.J. Bassett-Lowke [fig.36]. The geometric motifs he used in both relate not only to the designs of the Wiener Werkstätte (the design studio and workshops established in Vienna in 1903, to which Mackintosh was con-

Fig.32 | Arthur Melville *Autumn – Loch Lomond* 1893
Glasgow Museums: Kelvingrove Art Gallery and Museum

Fig.33 | David Gauld *St Agnes* 1889
National Gallery of Scotland, Edinburgh

Fig.34 | George Henry *A Galloway Landscape* 1889
Glasgow Museums: Kelvingrove Art Gallery and Museum

nected), but also to Art Deco. There is much in Mackintosh's French paintings which recall that diverse aesthetic. The views of Port Vendres, for example, his most frequent subject while in France, commonly use the favourite Art Deco motifs of broad bands or blocks of colour, and geometrical stylisation of natural forms. Finding pattern in nature had been a preoccupation throughout Mackintosh's career in his work in all media, and his French paintings are no exception; in watercolours such as *La Rue du Soleil* [plate 16], he must have delighted in the effect created by the reflections of quayside buildings, and freely exercised his graphic ability to produce an artwork where his predominant interest has been the visual pattern created by the rippling water.

In moving to the warm south of France, Mackintosh was in tune with a wider, fashionable belief in the health-giving benefits of the sun, enjoyed away from industrialised cities. This was extensively expressed in the art of the period, most explicitly through Art Deco motifs such as the sunburst. Hand in hand with this was a developing interest in the exotic and the attraction of 'primitive' and foreign cultures, which fed design styles of the period. This could be experienced in Port Vendres which, because of its position and its deep-water harbour, was the principal French port for Algeria. Mackintosh clearly enjoyed the busy life of the town and expressed this most poetically in *The Chronycle*, the series of letters he wrote to his wife while she was in London in 1927.[3]

Since the 1880s France had been a destination for Scottish artists, but they had tended to centre on Paris until figures such as Melville and then J.D. Fergusson and S.J. Peploe began to explore the Mediterranean coast. Fergusson in particular was one of the first British artists to come into direct contact with the important artistic developments taking place in France in the first decade of the twentieth century, an experience which transformed his art. From Paris (where he had settled in 1907) Fergusson moved to the French Mediterranean coast, but was forced to return to London at the beginning of the First World War. At the outbreak of hostilities Mackintosh was in Walberswick on the Suffolk coast. His architectural partnership with Honeyman & Keppie had recently been dissolved and he and Margaret had gone to Walberswick on holiday, where he was preoccupied with painting, producing numerous flower studies and a few landscapes [see figs.18–20]. By the following summer the Mackintoshes were in London, settling in Chelsea, close to Fergusson and his partner, the dancer Margaret Morris. There, Morris had established a dance school, which also operated as a social club, soon regularly attended by the Mackintoshes as well as by artists such as Randolph Schwabe, Augustus John, Jacob Epstein and Wyndham Lewis. During the early years of the First World War, in part because of the harsh new order it created, fierce divisions developed between artists that resulted in a cultural period that was both energetic and turbulent. This was exemplified by the exhibition *Twentieth Century Art: A Review of Modern Movements*, held at the Whitechapel Art Gallery in London in the early summer of 1914. This drew attention to a diversity of grouping including Walter Sickert and the Camden Town Group, the Bloomsbury painters, the rebellious Vorticists (of which Epstein and Lewis were part), and artists such as Stanley Spencer and Mark Gertler. Fergusson and Peploe also took part. If Mackintosh had not seen the exhibition, he must have become

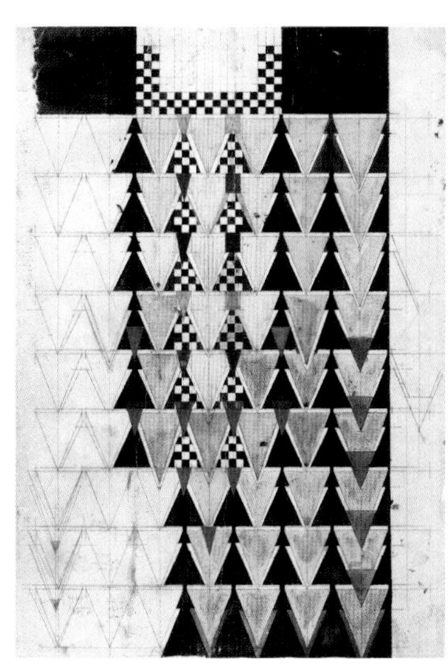

LEFT TO RIGHT

Fig.35 | Arthur Melville
A Sapphire Sea 1892
Private collection courtesy of Bourne Fine Art, Edinburgh

Fig.36 | C.R. Mackintosh
Design for a stencil for the hall of 78 Derngate, Northampton 1916
Hunterian Art Gallery, University of Glasgow

Fig.37 | C.R. Mackintosh
Textile design: Basket of Flowers c.1915–20
Hunterian Art Gallery, University of Glasgow

aware of these developments on his arrival in London. Later, with Fergusson, he was directly involved in this scene through the revival of the London Salon of Independents, serving on its management committee alongside the sculptor Frank Dobson and the critic Frank Rutter, whom he subsequently hoped would write on his French paintings.[4]

During the London years, in addition to the small amount of architectural design work undertaken, Mackintosh and his wife collaborated on at least one work, *The Voices of the Wood*, which was shown at the 1916 Arts and Crafts Exhibition Society. That work remains closer in sentiment to the Symbolism and fantasy of the couple's collaborations during their Glasgow period, but the Mackintoshes' wartime textile designs have a boldness informed by the angular graphic language of the Vorticists [fig.37]. Mackintosh's advertising designs undertaken for Bassett-Lowke's engineering company are of particular interest in this context [fig.38], sharing the diagonal orientation and mechanised imagery of Edward Wadsworth's woodcuts, which had been shown in London in 1919 [fig.39]. Mackintosh's interest in the abstract potential of industrial forms went no further, however. The most resolved paintings produced during his London years were the series of around ten watercolours showing flowers, such as *Begonias* [fig.40], each made with a high degree of finish.

As the First World War neared an end there developed among British artists a renewed interest in landscape painting. This came about partly through the move of a number of the most prominent artists to rural locations, for example, Duncan Grant and Vanessa Bell, who settled at Charleston in Sussex in 1916. Figures such as Paul Nash and Matthew Smith moved from London to the countryside to recuperate from their injuries or from stress caused by the war. Others such as Ben and Winifred Nicholson were now free to travel abroad, spending time in Switzerland, in the early 1920s, and then later in that decade basing themselves in Cumbria and then St Ives. In this way, some of the most progressive British artists of the period redirected their attention to the landscape, using it as a principal means for their artistic expression and, in so doing, contributed to a revitalisation of British landscape painting. While it may be too simplistic to describe this tendency as a step back from the radicalism which had fired British art in the early years of the twentieth century, British painting in the 1920s was by comparison uncontroversial in its choice of subject, retreating from demonstrably modern subjects in favour of more traditional motifs.

Mackintosh's developing interest in landscape painting can be better understood in this wider artistic context, as well as in response to the difficulties he was continuing to experience as a designer. Through his friendship with the Slade School-trained artist, Randolph Schwabe, he would have been aware of a type of conservative topographical draughtsmanship which valued the discipline of nineteenth-century English drawing and watercolour painting. We know of no other Mackintosh landscape paintings produced between those done in Dorset in 1920 [figs.21–24] and his move to France, but his interest in the potential of landscape motifs is clear in the comments he made about Fergusson's Scottish paintings of 1922, such as *Glen Isla* [fig.41]:

LEFT TO RIGHT

Fig.38 | C.R. Mackintosh
Advertising label for Bassett-Lowke Ltd c.1919
Hunterian Art Gallery, University of Glasgow

Fig.39 | Edward Wadsworth
The Open Window c.1915
Tate, London 2005

Fig.40 | C.R. Mackintosh
Begonias 1916
Private collection

Fig.41 | J.D. Fergusson
In Glen Isla 1922/3
University of Stirling J.D. Fergusson Memorial Collection

Fig.42 | Edward Wadsworth
Fortune's Well, Portland 1921
Manchester City Art Galleries

I have not forgotten the impressions they had on me when we saw them at Chelsea. I still have such a vivid mental picture of them that I can pass them in review one by one making a sort of subconscious 'peep-show' and see them quite clearly just as you showed them to us.[5]

Fergusson was only one of many artists, and by this time one of the less radical, who was producing work in this manner, that is to say making paintings based on a geometrical ordering of landscape motifs. At Dymchurch on the Kent coast in 1920, Paul Nash produced oils and fully resolved watercolours based on his exploration of the formal relationship between shoreline and sea, which have come to be viewed as a vital part in the development of English abstraction. Mackintosh was aware of Nash's work, drawing his wife's attention to an exhibition by the artist, held in London in 1927.[6]

Edward Wadsworth, whose wartime work was frequently based on mechanised imagery, had also become interested in the rural landscape and had developed a plan for a series of designs showing English ports, which he visited while walking from Cornwall to London in 1921. His stylised, cubistic paintings, such as *Fortune's Well, Portland* [fig.42], and of Marseilles (where he stayed in 1921), were shown at The Leicester Galleries in London in the spring of 1923. At the beginning of that year, Fergusson's close associates Peploe, Cadell and Hunter shared a joint exhibition there. By that time Peploe and Cadell had become regular visitors to the Hebridean island of Iona, where they produced painterly but carefully constructed views of its topography and its buildings [fig.43]. Later in 1923, in all probability for the first time since the First World War, Fergusson and Cadell returned to the south of France, painting at Antibes and Cassis and producing works which express not only their enthusiasm for the brilliant light and colour of the Mediterranean coast, but also their interest in the formal qualities of structure and pattern. It is hard to view works such as Fergusson's *Christmas Time in the South of France* and Cadell's paintings of Cassis [figs.44 & 45] without thinking of Mackintosh's own subsequent experience in France and the stylistic affinity between all these artists' paintings. Each was flourishing after the depression of the war years.

In choosing the most westerly point of the French Mediterranean coast, Mackintosh was at a remove from Fergusson and his fellow artists, Peploe, Cadell and Hunter (subsequently to become known as the Scottish Colourists), whose preference was for Provence and the Côte d'Azur. Although they first stayed at Amélie-les-Bains in the foothills of the Pyrénées, by 1924 the Mackintoshes found themselves a base at Port Vendres on the Côte Vermeille, adjacent to the fishing village of Collioure. Signac had painted there in 1887, followed some years later, in 1905, by Matisse and Derain. Inspired by the intimate atmosphere of the village, they worked experimentally and with an expressive freedom in their application of paint that led to them being dubbed 'Les Fauves' (wild beasts) [fig.46]. Part of their attraction to Collioure was in the village's 'undiscovered', rustic character which found an equivalent in their art, with its broken brushstrokes and raw colour; but for Derain, the most important thing was the *blond, golden light, which suppresses the shadows…*[7] Collioure remained a motif in Matisse's work into the 1910s, contributing to other artists' interest in the area. The lesser known Fauves, Alfred Marquet, Henri Manguin

and Charles Camoin, followed Matisse and Derain there soon after; Picasso and Braque (while in their Cubist phase) worked at nearby Céret between 1911 and 1913, where they were joined by Juan Gris, Auguste Herbin and Jean Marchand among others. Thus the area grew in interest to artists but never with the same level of popularity as the Côte d'Azur, and by the time of Mackintosh's arrival villages such as Collioure remained much as they had been in the nineteenth century, dependent on fishing for a livelihood and with few facilities for visitors.

During the 1920s, the waves of artistic activity in the area represented first by Matisse and Derain and then by Picasso and Braque had passed, although artists continued to visit and settle there. Chaïm Soutine painted at Céret at the beginning of that decade, while Collioure remained a particular focus for artists. Two English painters based there, Rudolph Ihlee and Edgar Hereford, had been known to Mackintosh from the years spent in London, and while Mackintosh met with them in France, *The Chronycle* provides us with a sense that he did not always wish their company.[8] His time with them appears to have been spent largely in a social way, dining or listening to gramophone music together, filling occasional evenings while he was parted from his wife. Little is mentioned of any artistic exchange, although Hereford lent Mackintosh books on Matisse and on the sculptor Aristide Maillol, whose home town was Banyuls-sur-Mer, a short distance down the coast. Hereford's painting remains largely unknown. Ihlee's work [see fig.7] has similarities to Mackintosh's but this is more likely a consequence of their shared surroundings and the strong Mediterranean light under which they were working, than any joint artistic intention. Mackintosh wished for no side by side relationship of the sort that had inspired Matisse and Derain twenty years earlier, and instead made it clear that he preferred working in solitude. Margaret would come to meet her husband only at the end of a working session at a prearranged point; Mackintosh indicates his distaste for those painters who seemed to seek an audience by practicing their art on the quays, and expresses his disquiet at being surrounded by a group of children while at work.[9]

Of other artists in the area, it is likely he would have been aware of the Frenchman Augustin Hanicotte, who had come to Collioure in 1915, and who in 1925 had started a drawing school for children, Les Gosses de Collioure, that often operated in the open air. In this way Hanicotte must have been one of the most prominent local artistic figures, through his teaching and his own work. Although Hanicotte's art has a monumentality familiar in Mackintosh's paintings, the foreground of his compositions are invariably filled with the busy activity of fishermen landing their catch [fig.47]. Mackintosh's works, by comparison, are devoid of people, while his views of Port Vendres – despite his enjoyment of the busy port's daily life – are largely empty of shipping, concentrating instead on the relationship between buildings and the settings they occupy. In the way that Mackintosh more generally referred to a wish not to be 'drawn out of my charming seclusion' in France, this seems to reflect the manner in which he went about his work.[10] Isolated spots where he was unlikely to be disturbed suited both his personal mood and his compositional needs as he tried for an art that was different from others.[11] In *The Chronycle* his references to

non-British artists are rare, limited to passing, disparaging comments on the French painters André Dunoyer de Segonzac, who was known to Fergusson, and Marie Laurencin, who worked in a cubistic style.[12] Of greater interest to him was news of artist friends such as the Scot, James Pryde, whom he is known to have admired and who specialised in paintings of buildings and monuments of dour mood.[13] Mackintosh was in correspondence with the Belgian artist Georges Marie Baltus (a teacher at Glasgow School of Art from 1906 to 1916) who, Mackintosh implies, saw his one work included in the British Artist's Exhibition, held at the Galérie Georges Petit in Paris in the spring of 1927, *Le Fort Mauresque* [plate 22][14]. Of particular pleasure was the news of J.D. Fergusson's approval of the French paintings Macdonald had returned to London with in 1927: 'I dont think that artistically [*sic*] there is any artist I would like to please better than Fergusson and Margaret Morris also…'.[15]

Mackintosh had hoped that Fergusson and Morris would spend time with him and his wife in France, but there is no record that such a visit happened. The lifestyle which Mackintosh and Macdonald followed there, in what proved to be the late years of their lives, was one of privacy. While Mackintosh's wide, earlier experience may have contributed much to shaping the paintings he subsequently made in France, a reading of the *The Chronycle* suggests that Mackintosh remained apart from local artistic influence and strongly independent in his wider views. He did not work in a spontaneous way, but relied on lengthy reflection and a prolonged working method, carried out across days and weeks. The decision to remain in France to paint provided a means of expressing himself without the difficulties which seemed insurmountable in his career as an architect. Writing in judgment of this phase in his art, he expressed a belief that, although he experienced crises of confidence, he had produced works of originality.[16] Just as it is possible to identify the numerous sources that contributed to his design work, so it is with his final paintings. But in both, ultimately we are left with a strong sense of Mackintosh's respect for nature and his profound response to its forms. Throughout his oeuvre, not least in these last watercolours, he deals with nature in a way which acknowledges the essential, life-giving importance of that source, which he represents with such individual invention that his art remains quite distinct from that of his contemporaries.

LEFT TO RIGHT

Fig.43 | F.C.B. Cadell *Iona, Croft* 1925–30
Scottish National Gallery of Modern Art, Edinburgh

Fig.44 | J. D. Fergusson *Christmas Time in the South of France* c.1923
The Fergusson Gallery, Perth and Kinross Council

Fig.45 | F.C.B. Cadell *Cassis* 1923/4
Private collection

Fig.46 | André Derain *Collioure* 1905
Scottish National Gallery of Modern Art, Edinburgh

Fig.47 | Augustin Hanicotte *Les voiles blanches* 1925
Galeries Raymonde Duval

VALLEYS & HILLS

The Pyrénées-Orientales are transversed by the river valleys of the rivers Têt and the Tech. These flow from the snow-covered mountain peaks to the coastal plain, the river banks punctuated by towns and villages. The Mackintoshes explored the region thoroughly, basing themselves variously at Amélie-les-Bains and Ille-sur-Têt, from where they sought out remote hamlets and churches, and subjects to paint.

Though dating back to Roman times, Amélie-les-Bains flourished from the nineteenth century as one of the largest and finest thermal springs in the area. Warm, sulphurous water flowed freely, servicing the Roman baths, the Pujade baths (1840), and a military hospital (1855). Margaret Macdonald described its ready availability to Jessie Newbery, 'Here there is no lack – both drinking + boiling sulphur water –the latter simply flows down the street gutter + one can always get a can of beautiful hot water without the trouble of heating. It is lovely for washing – especially one's hair.' The waters had particular benefits for rheumatism and respiratory complaints, but it is not known if either of the Mackintoshes took them for health reasons. The village of Amélie also enjoyed an exceptionally mild and sunny climate, sheltered from the whiplash of the tramontane winds. Margaret Macdonald again wrote to Jessie Newbery, 'This is quite a beautiful spot – in the valley of the Tech – so we are sheltered from the Tramontane – but we get the snow-wind off Canigou if the wind is from her direction – this, in spite of the glorious sun always gives a sharpness to the air which is rather exhilarating.' No paintings of Amélie itself are known, but from there Mackintosh could make the short walk to nearby Palalda, a picturesque hillside village which tumbles down to the river Tech. Records of it date back to the ninth century, and its two round towers are remnants of a thirteeth-century castle.

Ille-sur-Têt is a historic medieval town of narrow streets and vestigial fortifications. One visitor described some of its architectural surprises:

> *a great door that one would come suddenly upon, seen in a marble doorway in one of the sunless alleys, belonging to a house with Spanish traditions and opening into a courtyard, out of which a wide staircase with shallow steps would lead to a gallery and rooms with heavy woodwork and thick walls. Dignified houses, in spite of the restricted streets they flanked, coats of arms, since defaced, over the doorways, brass knockers, and great handles on the doors ... Than again, walking along the little streets one would be confronted with a fragment of sculpture built into the wall of a house ...*[1]

Mackintosh called it 'our beloved Ille-sur-Têt'. The couple stayed in the Hôtel du Midi, a simple, cheap hotel with good food and attentive staff. Mackintosh sent his friend, J.D. Fergusson, an amusing account of the dining room:

> *The eating room is a delightful feature. At the end is a long table the full length of the room at which the workmen sit. There are usually 6, 10 or 12 splendid fellows sitting here having a gorgeous feast and discussing the affairs of the world. It somehow reminds me of the Last Supper only there is no frugality here and the wine flows in a way that would have given life and gaiety to Leonardo's popular masterpiece.*[2]

Mackintosh found two subjects nearby. One was Bouleternère, another picturesque village on the banks of the Tech, dating back to the eleventh century. Two round towers are all that remains of its original medieval walls. In the seventeenth century its Romanesque church was surmounted with a new building, forming the church of St Sulpice, which crowns the hill top. The other subject was the striking limestone formations that punctuate the surrounding area and are known variously as Les Orgues [The Organs] or Les Demoiselles d'Ille. Mackintosh recorded one impressive formation located just to the north-west of the town.

Fig. 48 | Palalda from the north bank of the River Tech
Robin Crichton

1 PALALDA, PYRÉNÉES-ORIENTALES

CATALOGUE NOTE

The catalogue includes all of C.R. Mackintosh's recorded French paintings. Dates are given only when they are inscribed on the works. The support for the watercolours was often paper, pasted to a millboard backing .These boards may have been bought pre-prepared or, more likely, were assembled by Mackintosh himself. Dimensions are given in centimetres, height before width. The exhibition history of each watercolour is given to 1933, the year of the *Mackintosh Memorial Exhibition* held in Glasgow. Mackintosh's French watercolours were published in Roger Billcliffe, *Mackintosh Watercolours*, London, 1977, and these catalogue numbers are given here with the abbreviation RB. Additional works since located are listed in Pamela Robertson (ed.), *The Chronycle*, Glasgow 2001, and appear here with the abbreviation PR. Dated references refer to Mackintosh's letters in *The Chronycle*. Photographs of untraced works are reproduced from the record photographs of the 1933 exhibition. Where possible, each entry includes a recent black and white photograph showing the subject of Mackintosh's painting.

Signed: C.R. Mackintosh
Pencil and watercolour, 51.5 × 51.5
Exhibited: *Charles Rennie Mackintosh, Margaret Macdonald Mackintosh, Memorial Exhibition*, McLellan Galleries, Glasgow 1933 (74)
Checklist number 38 [RB 200]
Private collection, on loan to the Scottish National Gallery of Modern Art, Edinburgh

Mackintosh recorded Palalda from a low viewpoint on the other side of the Tech from the town. This allowed him to accentuate the verticality of its hillside location and offered a varied skyline. The overall grey tonality of the image is punctuated by occasional notes of deep sienna and vivid green. Mackintosh changed the red tiles of the roofs to dark grey to fit his sombre scheme.

Palalda

2 BOULETERNÈRE

Signed: C.R.M.
Pencil and watercolour, 44.7 × 44.7
Exhibited: *Charles Rennie Mackintosh, Margaret Macdonald Mackintosh, Memorial Exhibition*, McLellan Galleries, Glasgow 1933 (136)
Checklist number 39 [RB 201]
Donald and Eleanor Taffner, New York

This painting is a compilation of two different views of Bouleternère. The upper half consists of a view of the church and its surrounding buildings from a relatively low viewpoint. Below that Mackintosh has pasted in an additional strip showing a straight-on view of the town and its connecting bridge. In reality this is a separate view from a vantage point a few hundred yards to the west. In amalgamating the two views, Mackintosh gives modest Bouleternère dramatic presence by exaggerating its verticality and positioning the imposing round tower in the centre of the composition. In Palalda, and especially here in Bouleternère, the staring, open-shuttered windows provide a slightly unsettling sense of being watched. The apparently haphazard composition has been composed with great care. A dominant white façade has been carefully placed at the centre of the composition; indeed, its chimney is at its very heart.

Bouleternère, showing the two different views of the village used by Mackintosh

3 HÉRÉ-DE-MALLET, ILLE-SUR-TÊT

Pencil and watercolour, 46 × 46
Exhibited: *Charles Rennie Mackintosh, Margaret Macdonald Mackintosh, Memorial Exhibition*, McLellan Galleries, Glasgow 1933 (53, as Margaret Macdonald Mackintosh)
Checklist number 40 [RB 204]
Private collection, on loan to the Scottish National Gallery of Modern Art, Edinburgh

Mackintosh has intensified the colours of the rock and shadows, and emphasised the horizontal banding in the stone. The crown of the rock sits above the rock face like a simplified Vauban fort, or a Mackintosh castle, and evokes his early sketch of Stirling Castle [fig.11].

Héré-de-Mallet, Ille-sur-Têt

4 A HILL TOWN IN SOUTHERN FRANCE

Pencil and watercolour, 42 × 42
Exhibited: *Charles Rennie Mackintosh, Margaret Macdonald Mackintosh, Memorial Exhibition*, McLellan Galleries, Glasgow 1933 (44)
Checklist number 41 [RB 191]
Private collection, courtesy of Christie's

This subject has not been identified. The topography is not characteristic of the Pyrénées-Orientales and it is possible that this painting was made on a trip outside of the area, perhaps to Spain. The handling of the watercolour is looser and the colour more flamboyant than in the other watercolours. The sky, for example, is not a flat blue but streaked with tones of blue and indigo.

FARMHOUSES

Mackintosh was drawn to the simple but substantial farm buildings of the Têt and Tech valleys, with their straightforward, functional construction, usually of stone and mortar, and red-tiled roofs, which combined living quarters for the owners and employees, working space for the farm, and accommodation for the animals. He would have admired the fact that the buildings had evolved out of local need and local materials. In his student days he had extolled similar virtues in his architectural writings and sought to follow them in his built work.

This surviving group of five paintings may well all date from the earlier part of the Mackintoshes' time in France. In January 1925, Margaret Macdonald had written to Jessie Newbery 'You think, as we do – about Dorset – It is quite the best in every way – this comes very near to it + the buildings are a perpetual joy to us. Toshie is going to paint some of the 'maas' as they call them – farmhouses really – so you will see what they are like some day – I hope.'
Two of the farms have been identified: one on the outskirts of Amélie-les-Bains, and one just outside Ille.

The watercolours all show a solitary farm set at a shallow angle to the viewer and occupying the upper section of the composition. It is as if the artist wanted to draw attention to the interdependent relationship between these buildings and the land which gave the farmers work and from which the buildings were made. The occupants, whose activity shaped the appearance of the land, are never shown.

The Têt and Tech valleys provided productive farmland. An account of 1931 provides a useful description of the varied cultivation made possible by irrigation:

In the plains of Roussillon derivation canals from the Têt and Tech irrigate large areas and the cultivation of the vine, early vegetables and fruits in the huertas of the Rivieral in the lower Têt valley and of Bas Valespir along the Tech, are very profitable. Melons, aubergines, and tomatoes, early potatoes, celery and all kinds of vegetables are grown, sheltered by lines of reeds and fruit trees from the tramontane. These are sent to the great distributing market of Perpignan ...[3]

The Mackintoshes would have been aware of the seasonal activity of the countryside, and of the bustling local markets, such as that at Ille where they stayed in 1925. *The Chronycle* records their pleasure of the local fresh produce. Mackintosh regularly provides details of meals served at the Hôtel du Commerce, commenting on the cheese, fish, meat, and especially his favourite cherries from Céret, 'semi-wild little things full of suggestion'.

Fig. 49 | Domaine de Saint-Jean à Perpignan from *L'Architecture Rurale en Languedoc en Roussillon*, Espace Sud Editions et C. Lhuisset, Montpellier, 1992

5 MONT ALBA

Pencil and watercolour, 38.7 × 43.8
Exhibited: *Charles Rennie Mackintosh, Margaret Macdonald Mackintosh, Memorial Exhibition*, McLellan Galleries, Glasgow 1933 (156)
Checklist number 42 [RB 189]
Scottish National Gallery of Modern Art, Edinburgh, purchased 1990

This isolated farm is a few kilometres south of Amélie-les-Bains, and was not easily reached by foot. Cars, and mules or horses with guides, were available for hire at Amélie. Mackintosh wrote in December 1925 of having visited the isolated and 'delicious small church' of Mont Alba. The Mackintoshes would have passed this farm on their way there, taking the road that can been seen sweeping across the foreground, disappearing round the corner, then reappearing over the bridge at centre back. The lack of growth in the fields suggests the painting was made in the late autumn or early part of the year.

Farmhouse at Montalba-d'Amélie

6 BLANC ONTOINE

Pencil and watercolour, 39.1 × 50.6
Exhibited: *Charles Rennie Mackintosh, Margaret Macdonald Mackintosh, Memorial Exhibition*, McLellan Galleries, Glasgow 1933 (40)
Checklist number 43 [RB 202]
Hunterian Art Gallery, University of Glasgow

'Blanc Ontoine' is a small farm outside Ille-sur-Têt, locally known as the Mas Blanc. It is situated on what was in the 1920s the main road to Bouleternère. The bare tree in the foreground and the wintry foliage behind suggest it was painted at the turn of the year. The farm has since been modernised, but is still recognisable. The sky is more expressively handled than in most of Mackintosh's watercolours, and recalls *A Hill Town in Southern France* [plate 4].

Blanc Ontoine, Ille-sur-Têt

7 A SPANISH FARM

Pencil and watercolour, 28 × 38
Exhibited: *Charles Rennie Mackintosh, Margaret Macdonald Mackintosh, Memorial Exhibition*, McLellan Galleries, Glasgow 1933 (154)
Checklist number 44 [RB 181]
Private collection

This subject has not been identified. The work was given this title for the 1933 *Mackintosh Memorial Exhibition*, but there is no corroboratory evidence on the painting itself, and none to suggest it is a Spanish subject. The lack of growth on the trees and vines, combined with the pink blossom, suggests a date of early spring, in February or March. In Port Vendres, during the hot summer, Mackintosh noted his admiration for the resourceful vine: 'Very remarkable are these vines – where they are the hills are a vivid green – next them [*sic*] where there is grass or other vegetation is grey yellow brown – everything is now dried up but the vines they must send their roots scuttling far and wide to pick up moisture.' (29 May, 9.1)

8 SUMMER IN THE SOUTH

Pencil and watercolour, 28.3 × 38.5
Exhibited: *Charles Rennie Mackintosh, Margaret Macdonald Mackintosh, Memorial Exhibition*, McLellan Galleries, Glasgow 1933 (138)
Checklist number 45 [RB 195]
Private collection, on loan to the Scottish National Gallery of Modern Art, Edinburgh

The subject is unidentified. Again, the presence of blossom suggests a date in spring.

9 A SOUTHERN FARM

Pencil and watercolour, 43.4 × 43.4
Exhibited: *Charles Rennie Mackintosh, Margaret Macdonald Mackintosh, Memorial Exhibition*, McLellan Galleries, Glasgow 1933 (56)
Checklist number 46 [RB 192]
Hunterian Art Gallery, University of Glasgow

The farm is unidentified. Mackintosh characteristically draws attention to modest details – the tethering post and ground worked by the absent farm animal, and the cockerel silhouetted in the open doorway.

8

COLLIOURE

The Mackintoshes found the pretty fishing village of Collioure soon after their arrival in France. Margaret Macdonald described it as 'one of the most wonderful places we have ever seen'.[4] It may be that, from 1924, the couple took hotel accommodation in Port Vendres, just a half-hour walk away along a coastal path, which offers breathtaking views of the Côte Vermeille. In *The Chronycle*, Mackintosh records regular walks to Collioure and visits to the two younger English painters, Rudolph Ihlee and Edgar Hereford, whom they knew from London and who had lodgings and studios in Collioure from 1922. Sociable evenings were spent with them and their landlady, having supper and listening to gramophone music in their studios.

Collioure sits at the edge of a sheltered double bay, on the Mediterranean coast near the Franco-Spanish border. Though small, it is dominated by a succession of striking landmarks which document its long and varied history: the Château des Templiers, first mentioned in 672 and from the twelfth to the seventeenth centuries occupied by the Kings of Majorca; Vauban's Fort Miradou of 1671 and other fortifications; the seventeenth-century church attached to its distinctive lighthouse/ bell tower which dates back to the thirteenth century: and, at the end of the breakwater, the little Chapel of St Vincent.

In the 1920s Collioure was largely undiscovered as a tourist destination, though artists had started to visit from the early 1900s. There was no hotel accommodation; the now-famous Hôtel des Templiers, for example, which opened in 1922, was then just a little café without even its terrace on the river. The two beaches which flanked the Château des Templiers were places of work not leisure, scenes of constant business as the small fishing boats plied in and out on their trade to the wider sea: nets were mended, sails dried, and sardines and other fish sold. Some of this activity is recorded in photographs and postcard views of the day, and in the paintings of the local artist, Augustin Hanicotte (1886–1971) [fig.47]. Today, Collioure bristles with yachts and tourists.

Three paintings by Mackintosh of the village survive: one of the massive front elevation of the château; the second, the Fort Miradou, brooding above the harbour; and the third, the facetted houses of a quiet corner near the beach. The church and its bell tower, which play such a significant role in the depictions of Matisse, Derain, and others, appear to have been ignored by Mackintosh.

Fig.50 | Postcard view of Collioure, showing fishing boats on the beach and, at the far end, the church of Notre-Dame-des-Anges
Archives Départmentales, Perpignan

Fig.51 | Postcard view of Collioure
Archives Départmentales, Perpignan

10 COLLIOURE, PYRÉNÉES-ORIENTALES – SUMMER PALACE OF THE QUEENS OF ARAGON

Signed: C.R. Mackintosh
Pencil and watercolour, 38.1 × 43.2
Exhibited: *Charles Rennie Mackintosh, Margaret Macdonald Mackintosh, Memorial Exhibition*, McLellan Galleries, Glasgow 1933 (42)
Checklist number 47 [RB 178]
The National Trust for Scotland, The Hill House

Mackintosh has recorded the imposing south elevation of the 'Summer Palace' in the morning, when the east light defined its buttresses and gables. His vantage point was an elevated position on the other side of the bay, just off the main road that links Port Vendres and Collioure. The foreground landmass is generalised. The modest hills in the background have been aggrandised, their curving forms and muted colours providing a complementary foil to the man-made fortified palace. The austere massing of the château must have evoked for him memories of the south elevation of the Glasgow School of Art.

Collioure, looking towards the Château des Templiers

C. R. MACKINTOSH

11 COLLIOURE

Pencil and watercolour, 37.9 × 46.5
Exhibited: *6th International Exhibition of Watercolor Painting*, The Art Institute of Chicago 1926 (316); *Charles Rennie Mackintosh, Margaret Macdonald Mackintosh, Memorial Exhibition*, McLellan Galleries, Glasgow 1933 (131)
Checklist number 48 [RB 179]
The Art Institute of Chicago

Mackintosh positioned himself close to the water's edge, across the bay from the main harbour, looking up at the seventeenth-century Fort Miradou. He has emphasised its defensive bastion, which projects into space like the prow of a ship. Only a select group of four fishing boats is included on the far shore. In *The Chronycle* Mackintosh decries his preference for green. Here, however, his painting resonates with vibrant shades of blue in the sea and shadows.

Collioure, looking towards the Fort Miradou

12 A SOUTHERN TOWN

Pencil and watercolour, 32.3 × 37.5
Exhibited: *Charles Rennie Mackintosh, Margaret Macdonald Mackintosh, Memorial Exhibition*, McLellan Galleries, Glasgow 1933 (142)
Checklist number 49 [RB 193]
Hunterian Art Gallery, University of Glasgow

This view shows the Place Jean Jaurès and the rue de la Democratie to the left. The late afternoon light creates long shadows across the façades, emphasising the buildings' angled roofline and gables, a theme Mackintosh also explored in the right-hand section of *Collioure* [plate 11]. By contrast the foreground and background landscape are broadly handled. Mackintosh gives a rare glimpse of human activity in the figures gathered at street tables outside the corner café.

Place Jean Jaurès and rue de la Democratie, Collioure

PORT VENDRES

Port Vendres can trace its roots back to the Romans, when it was the *Portus Veneris*. Its success has been founded on its deep and sheltered harbour, which has been successively developed over centuries. Major investment was carried out in the late eighteenth century, following the plans of Maréchal Mailly. These enlarged the port and gave the town a central square, dominated by an obelisk to Louis XVI, and the low-lying Fort Mailly on the outskirts of the town. A new church to Notre Dame de Bonne Nouvelle opened in 1888 and the lighthouse on Cap Béar was built in the early 1900s. In the 1930s, shortly after the Mackintoshes' visits, major expansion included the extension of the Quai de la Douane, including the construction of a new gare maritime. The rue du Soleil and much of the port was rebuilt after the destruction by German troops in 1944.

In the 1920s the harbour was dominated by the large ships that transported cargo and passengers between France and north Africa. Port Vendres then ranked as France's third most important Mediterranean port. Weekly sailings of great steamboats, such as the *Gouverneur Général Cambon*, departed for Algiers and Morocco. The ships carried cargos of flour and carob beans, wood and wine, and passengers: some 60,000 Africans then passed through Port Vendres each year.

The Mackintoshes took rooms in the Hôtel du Commerce, on the Quai du Commerce, now the Quai Pierre Forgas. From the vantage point of the street-level café/ restaurants or from their balconies, they would have had excellent observation points for the comings and goings of the port. Mackintosh regularly described for Margaret the ships' activities, during her absence in London:

> *Friday 13th May Four other ships have come in besides the 'Esperos' One is laden with wood (sweet smelling) One with copper ore One with what looks like Gold Dust I suppose it is sulphur and one has salted sardines &c which as not so nice as the Carubs [sic] Wood copper and gold – these all seem suitable merchandice to bring into this our beautiful sunlit harbour.* (13 May, 21.1)

Of the surviving French watercolours, almost half show Port Vendres and its buildings and harbour from different vantage points. However, the town's eighteenth-century developments and the recent church did not attract interest. Of the largely abandoned fortifications, which overlooked the town and included Fort St Elme, Fort Béar and Fort Mauresque, Mackintosh was principally fascinated with Fort Mailly. This modest structure, now ruined, sits on a low-lying hill to the south-east of Port Vendres. On one side is a narrow gully, on the other the sea. Mackintosh produced at least four watercolours, each from different vantage points, exploring its setting and relationship to the landscape.

Fig.52 | Postcard view of Port Vendres, looking across the harbour, c.1906
Archives Départmentales, Perpignan

Fig.53 | Postcard view of Port Vendres, showing the Quai Pierre Forgas. The Hôtel du Commerce, where the Mackintoshes stayed, is to the right of the bows of the 'Medjerda'
Archives Départmentales, Perpignan

13 A SOUTHERN PORT

60 Pencil and watercolour, 36.2 × 44.5
Exhibited: *Charles Rennie Mackintosh, Margaret Macdonald Mackintosh, Memorial Exhibition*, McLellan Galleries, Glasgow 1933 (150)
Checklist number 50 [RB 176]
Glasgow Museums: Kelvingrove Art Gallery and Museum

This early view looks north-east to the open sea, taking in the rue du Soleil on the left, and on the right (from left to right) the landmarks of Fort Mailly, Sidi Ferruch – an eighteenth-century mini-fort and gun emplacement, and the Quai de la Douane. The level of the quay has been dropped to let these features be seen. Mackintosh's vantage point was probably a balcony of the Hôtel du Commerce. A contemporary account provides an evocative description of a similar view:

> *The great 'three-master' moored to the quay under our hotel windows is a beautiful wooden ship, coppered as the old East Indiamen were. The ample bulk of her hull spreads in a broad swelling line, and she gives herself to the sea as though she loved it ... She has so much room, a stately deck to wander on and sit and enjoy. The slim white spars across her masts and the ropes and rigging knit together the airy framework overhead. She has brought karub beans, and the sweet smell of them is everywhere... [At night] The 'three-master' is heaving all the time. The harbour breathes and you feel her rising and falling with every breath. The harbour is alive.*[5]

Port Vendres, from the Hôtel du Commerce

14 PORT VENDRES

Pencil and watercolour, 28 × 39.6
Exhibited: *Charles Rennie Mackintosh, Margaret Macdonald Mackintosh, Memorial Exhibition*, McLellan Galleries, Glasgow 1933 (155)
Checklist number 51 [RB 209]
The British Museum, London

The Mackintoshes would have seen this straightforward view of the port buildings on the Quai de la Douane every time they left the Hôtel du Commerce. Mackintosh's vantage point was perhaps one of its balconies. The foreground buildings were warehouses for wood, wine and other cargo. Mackintosh commented on the quantity of imported wine coming into the port: 'This port is getting simply a deposit for Spanish Wine – it comes in so many boats that they cant clear it away in time for the next arrivals to discharge.' (3 June, 11.1)

Port Vendres, looking towards the Quai de la Douane

BOIS

15 PORT VENDRES, LA VILLE

Signed: C.R. Mackintosh
Pencil and watercolour, 46 × 46
Exhibited: *Charles Rennie Mackintosh, Margaret Macdonald Mackintosh, Memorial Exhibition*, McLellan Galleries, Glasgow 1933 (ex-cat.)
Checklist number 52 [RB 186]
Glasgow Museums: Kelvingrove Art Gallery and Museum

The composition shows a view of Port Vendres from above the rue du Soleil, looking to the Quai du Commerce and the Quai Pierre Forgas. The four-storey Hôtel du Commerce with its street awning can be picked out at the left. The horizontally 'banded' composition takes in the cultivated terraces, where Mackintosh was seated, the rooftops of the rue du Soleil, the harbour, the quays, and the hills beyond.

Port Vendres from above the rue du Soleil, looking to the Quai du Commerce and the Quai Pierre Forgas

C R MACKINTOSH

16 LA RUE DU SOLEIL

Signed and dated: C.R. Mackintosh 1927; dated verso 1926
Pencil and watercolour, 39.7 × 38.2
Exhibited: *Charles Rennie Mackintosh, Margaret Macdonald Mackintosh, Memorial Exhibition*, McLellan Galleries, Glasgow 1933 (47)
Checklist number 53 [RB 208]
Hunterian Art Gallery, University of Glasgow

The subject is the east end of the rue du Soleil, or rue Arago, on the north-west side of Port Vendres. This section of the harbour was substantially rebuilt after the Second World War. Mackintosh presents a direct view of the harbour edge, its ramparts and buildings. His focus was the striated patterns created by their reflections in the eddying sea. The work was sold by The Leicester Galleries, London, in 1928, although it cannot be said with any certainty that it was exhibited there at that time.

Rue du Soleil, Port Vendres

C.R.MACKINTOSH.1927

17 THE LITTLE BAY, PORT VENDRES

Signed and dated: C.R. Mackintosh 1927
Pencil and watercolour, 39.3 × 39.3
Exhibited: *Charles Rennie Mackintosh, Margaret Macdonald Mackintosh, Memorial Exhibition*, McLellan Galleries, Glasgow 1933 (50)
Checklist number 54 [RB 214]
Hunterian Art Gallery, University of Glasgow

For this complex view of Port Vendres, Mackintosh sat on a stairwell beside the Redouté du Fanal lighthouse. The stairwell can be seen to the left of *The Lighthouse* [plate 23]. From his elevated vantage point he looked down to a man-made platform and to the sheltered beach beneath, beyond that to the west end of the Quai Arago and the back of the rue du Soleil with, in the distance, the Quai de la Douane. He added an invented view of the town against the sky. The composition provides a strong sense of movement in and out of the picture frame, of high and low viewpoints. A sense of serenity is achieved through his use of pure colour washes and tight geometric patterns. The bollard in the foreground, a recycled cannon, is given the status of a still-life centrepiece. The work was sold by The Leicester Galleries, London, in 1928, although it cannot be said with any certainty that it was exhibited there at that time. The bay shown in the foreground is now filled in and occupied by a fish market.

C.R.MACKINTOSH 1927

18–21 STEAMERS

18 MEN UNLOADING A STEAMER AT THE QUAYSIDE

Crayon and watercolour, 25.3 × 21.1
Checklist number 55 [RB 213]
Hunterian Art Gallery, University of Glasgow

19 STEAMER MOORED AT THE QUAYSIDE

Crayon and watercolour, 25.3 × 21.1
Checklist number 56 [RB 210]
Hunterian Art Gallery, University of Glasgow

20 STEAMER AT THE QUAYSIDE

Crayon and watercolour, 25.2 × 21
Checklist number 57 [RB 212]
Hunterian Art Gallery, University of Glasgow

21 STEAMERS AT THE QUAYSIDE

Crayon and watercolour, 25.2 × 21
Checklist number 58 [RB 211]
Hunterian Art Gallery, University of Glasgow

View from the Quai Pierre Forgas towards the rue du Soleil, Port Vendres

This is a puzzling group of watercolours. Stylistically the four works bear little relationship to Mackintosh's documented French paintings. They are drawn freely with the brush. Three of them are on sheets of thin tracing paper, of the same quality and size that Mackintosh used for most of *The Chronycle*. The subject matter, of close-in details of Port Vendres's cargo ships, is not typical. The group was, perhaps, a one-off experiment, not repeated, or they may have been by another hand, given to Mackintosh, and subsequently formed part of the Mackintoshes' estate. The background of two of the works shows a simplified view of the rue du Soleil, suggesting the vantage point for all four may have been a balcony of the Hôtel du Commerce.

18

19

20

21

22 LE FORT MAURESQUE

Signed: C.R.M.
Watercolour, dimensions unrecorded
Exhibited: *British Artists' Exhibitions*, Galérie Georges Petit, Paris 1927 (102); *Charles Rennie Mackintosh, Margaret Macdonald Mackintosh, Memorial Exhibition*, McLellan Galleries, Glasgow 1933 (49)
Not exhibited [RB 183]
Untraced

This now largely ruined fort, to the north of Port Vendres, is dramatically located on the edge of the Anse Mauresque. In the picture, Mackintosh has swung the lighthouse and foreland from the other side of the harbour into the top right corner, effectively drawing the mouth of the harbour together.

23 THE LIGHTHOUSE

Signed: C.R. Mackintosh
Pencil and watercolour, 27 × 37.5
Checklist number 59 [PR 23]
Private collection, courtesy of The Fine Art Society, London

Port Vendres has two navigational lighthouses: one on the Cap Béar, the subject of this painting, and the other on the Redouté du Fanal. For this view, Mackintosh positioned himself on the coastal path of the Redouté Béar. The simplified forms of the curving path and rock face provide a powerful end stop to the composition. The Mackintoshes could see the lights of the lighthouses from their rooms in the Hôtel du Commerce. A lonely Mackintosh described them to his absent wife: 'One side of the harbour green light the other red light but no letter from Margaret – silver light.' (13 May, 2.5A)

The lighthouse on Cap Béar, seen from the Redouté Béar, Port Vendres

C.R.MACKINTOSH

24 THE ROAD THROUGH THE ROCKS

Signed: C.R. Mackintosh
Pencil and watercolour, 49.5 × 43
Exhibited: *Charles Rennie Mackintosh, Margaret Macdonald Mackintosh, Memorial Exhibition*, McLellan Galleries, Glasgow 1933 (57)
Not exhibited [RB 182]
Private collection

This is probably Mackintosh's earliest surviving view of Fort Mailly on the outskirts of Port Vendres. Perched on the Redouté Béar, Mackintosh looked straight at the main entrance of the fort. The rock formations, hills and cuttings, create a dynamic mass around the rigid structure of the low-slung fort. At this stage Mackintosh's handling of the sea is conventional. Mackintosh returned to a very similar view in his later watercolour, *The Fort* [plate 25].

Fort Mailly, Port Vendres

25 THE FORT

Signed: C.R. Mackintosh
Pencil and watercolour, 45.2 × 45.4
Exhibited: *Charles Rennie Mackintosh, Margaret Macdonald Mackintosh, Memorial Exhibition*, McLellan Galleries, Glasgow 1933 (39)
Checklist number 60 [RB 184]
Hunterian Art Gallery, University of Glasgow

Mackintosh's vantage point was a spot just beneath Sidi Ferruch, but slightly further to the east than in *The Road through the Rocks* [plate 24]. He rejected the lighthouse seen from that position in favour of the more substantial white lighthouse on the other side of the harbour, on the Redouté du Fanal. He would have turned ninety degrees to the west to get the view of it shown here together with the distant view of the Côte Vermeille, which he placed on the horizon. The fortified base of the lighthouse, seen in *The Lighthouse* [plate 23], was replaced with a rocky outcrop.

Fort Mailly, Port Vendres

C R MACKINTOSH

26 LE FORT MAILLERT

Signed and dated: C.R. Mackintosh 1927
Pencil and watercolour, 35.8 × 28.5
Charles Rennie Mackintosh, Margaret Macdonald Mackintosh, Memorial Exhibition, McLellan Galleries, Glasgow 1933 (102)
Checklist number 61 [RB 215]
Glasgow School of Art

Two views are combined here: a view of Fort Mailly from a position directly opposite the fort, on the other side of the gully, and a lower vantage point of the rock face. As in his view of the Summer Palace of the Queens of Aragon [plate 10], Mackintosh contrasts the faceted striations of the rock formation with the clean, white, almost modernist elevations of the fort.

Fort Mailly, Port Vendres

C.R. MACKINTOSH 1927

27 PORT VENDRES

Signed: C.R. Mackintosh
Pencil and watercolour, 28.8 × 39.6
Exhibited: *Charles Rennie Mackintosh, Margaret Macdonald Mackintosh, Memorial Exhibition*, McLellan Galleries, Glasgow 1933 (135)
Checklist number 62 [RB 185]
Private collection, courtesy of The Fine Art Society, London

This view shows the other side of Fort Mailly, looking back to Port Vendres. Mackintosh has greatly increased the scale and height of the fort and its base. The background hills have been excised to allow the fort to be seen silhouetted against a brilliant blue sky.

Fort Mailly and Port Vendres, viewed from the east

28 THE ROCK

Signed and dated: C.R. Mackintosh 1927
Pencil and watercolour, 30.5 × 36.8
Exhibited: *Charles Rennie Mackintosh, Margaret Macdonald Mackintosh, Memorial Exhibition*, McLellan Galleries, Glasgow 1933 (130)
Checklist number 63 [RB 216]
Private collection

The painting of *The Rock* is regularly documented in *The Chronycle*. This striking, but modest cluster of lightly metamorphosed siltstone sits in Anse Béar, and is now cut into by a new walkway. Mackintosh would have passed it on his regular visits to Fort Mailly. The striations of the rocks have been simplified into bold patterns. The foreground suggests a sandy shore where none exists. The background is a view of Port Vendres, looking more to the south-west, with the rue du Soleil stretching into the middle distance at left, and the shore and boats seen in *The Little Bay* [plate 17] to the right.

The rocks at Anse Béar, with Port Vendres in the background

C.R. MACKINTOSH 1927

MOUNTAINS

The summer heat forced many, including the Mackintoshes, away from the coast. A favourite destination of theirs, which they visited at least twice, was Mont Louis, a small town high in the Pyrénées, some 5,000 feet above sea level. The pure air and healthy lifestyle clearly suited the couple. Mackintosh wrote to Margaret Macdonald, 'You know what a wonderful atmosphere you get there and with lots of rest and some simple and delightful walks with me to make the pace you will soon be the charming bounding chamois that you have always been.' (19 June, 20A)

Mont Louis has the distinction of being the highest garrison town in France, and is distinguished for its remarkably intact ramparts and dry moats built by Vauban in 1681. One visitor described her exhilarating train journey there and the town:

We came up to the Cerdagne by the most amazing little electric railway; it flew across the Têt and plunged into tunnels every few yards. Sometimes the river has been pushed out of its bed to build the line: in twenty three miles we rose nearly three thousand feet.

Mont Louis, built on this high edge by the French when they took the Cerdagne over, is every stone of it seventeenth century: just a little fort all to itself, walled and gated and fossed.

Our hotel (Figaro) abutted on the outer wall, looking out over the broad grassy terrace of the further side of the moat where white poplars stand sentinel: our bedroom walls were seven feet thick: always the feeling of a fortress. The sight of soldiers reminded one that Mont Louis is still a garrison town.

At Mont Louis you are right on the edge of the Cerdagne, well up it is true, on a great broad undulating pasture-country, set round with mountains.[6]

In the late 1920s there were three hotels in Mont Louis, the Jambon, the Hôtel de France, and the Hôtel des Pyrénées, run by M. Figaro, where the Mackintoshes also stayed. Mackintosh did not paint Mont Louis, but, instead, found subjects in the surrounding landscape and plants [see plates 39–44], and in the modest hamlets of nearby Fetges and La Llagonne. These little communities were analysed by Mackintosh with the same intensity with which he explored Port Vendres. Three views of Fetges are known, and four of La Llagonne, all from different vantage points.

Fig.54 | Postcard view of Mont Louis
Club Catalan

29 SLATE ROOFS

Signed: C.R. Mackintosh
Pencil and watercolour, 37 × 27.8
Exhibited: *Charles Rennie Mackintosh, Margaret Macdonald Mackintosh, Memorial Exhibition*, McLellan Galleries, Glasgow 1933 (94)
Checklist number 64 [RB 194]
Glasgow School of Art

Fetges sits east of and below Mont Louis. *Slate Roofs* shows a view of the village taken from just outside the entrance to Mont Louis, looking across the Têt valley. Mackintosh's technique, in this early work, depends on generous strokes of the loaded brush rather than the precise draughtsmanship and careful application of pigment found in his later works.

Fetges

C.R. MACKINTOSH

30 FETGES

Signed: C.R. Mackintosh
Pencil and watercolour, 46.5 × 45.8
Exhibited: Society of Scottish Artists, Edinburgh 1928 (36)
Checklist number 65 [RB 180]
Tate: Presented by Walter W. Blackie 1929

This wider, more detailed view of Fetges takes in the full village. It clearly expresses the roadside vantage point which Mackintosh used here and for *Slate Roofs*. Mackintosh believed this to be one of his finest works, declaring 'I shall probably never do its like again.' (11 June, 15.1) *Fetges* was one of the group of paintings Margaret Macdonald took with her to London in 1927 to try to raise interest in Mackintosh's work. The work was subsequently presented by Walter Blackie, his patron at The Hill House, to the Tate Gallery, London.

C.R.MACKINTOSH

31 MOUNTAIN VILLAGE

Signed: C.R.M.
Watercolour (dimensions unrecorded)
Exhibited: *Charles Rennie Mackintosh, Margaret Macdonald Mackintosh, Memorial Exhibition*, McLellan Galleries, Glasgow 1933 (161)
Not exhibited [RB 199]
Untraced

Mountain Village is also of Fetges, taken from a hillside vantage point above and to the west of the village and looking down the Têt valley. The dominant foreground building is the block with open spaces seen at the left of both *Fetges* and *The Boulders*. The composition offers an uncharacteristic sense of receding space.

32 THE BOULDERS

Signed: C.R.M.
Pencil and watercolour, 33.3 × 38
Exhibited: *Charles Rennie Mackintosh, Margaret Macdonald Mackintosh, Memorial Exhibition*, McLellan Galleries, Glasgow 1933 (46)
Checklist number 66 [RB 177]
Hunterian Art Gallery, University of Glasgow

The Boulders, again, shows Fetges. Mackintosh has combined three views: one showing the upper village from slightly further north than *Slate Roofs* and *Fetges*; one a near-to view of the principal yellow block which sits on the roadside; and finally a rocky outcrop, probably taken from below the road.

Fetges, viewed from above the road from Mont Louis

33 THE POOR MAN'S VILLAGE

Watercolour (dimensions unrecorded)
Exhibited: *Charles Rennie Mackintosh, Margaret Macdonald Mackintosh, Memorial Exhibition*, McLellan Galleries, Glasgow 1933 (38)
Not exhibited [RB 190]
Untraced

This view of La Llagonne is taken from near the rock formation shown in *The Village of La Llagonne*. Mackintosh has exaggerated the rise of the town on its gentle hillside.

34 THE VILLAGE OF LA LLAGONNE

Signed: C.R. Mackintosh
Pencil and watercolour, 45.7 × 45.7
Exhibited: *Charles Rennie Mackintosh, Margaret Macdonald Mackintosh, Memorial Exhibition*, McLellan Galleries, Glasgow 1933 (58)
Checklist number 67 [RB 188]
Glasgow Museums: Kelvingrove Art Gallery and Museum

Mackintosh's vantage point was looking north from the path beneath the church [see plates 33 & 35]. This is another composite of two views taken from one spot. The foreground architecture has been accurately rendered, though the yellow building, centre left, either no longer survives or has been brought in from the left. The distinctive rock formation in the middle ground is in reality situated to the west.

Rock formations at La Llagonne

La Llagonne

C.R. MACKINTOSH

35 THE CHURCH OF LA LLAGONNE

Signed: C.R. Mackintosh
Pencil and watercolour, 28 × 38.3
Exhibited: *Charles Rennie Mackintosh, Margaret Macdonald Mackintosh, Memorial Exhibition*, McLellan Galleries, Glasgow 1933 (160)
Checklist number 68 [RB 187]
Private collection

This view is taken from the east. The land slopes away from La Llagonne and does not allow the slightly elevated viewpoint Mackintosh gives here.

La Llagonne

C.R.MACKINTOSH

36 MOUNTAIN LANDSCAPE

Signed: C.R. Mackintosh
Pencil and watercolour, 25 × 35
Not exhibited [RB 198]
Untraced and unphotographed

37 MOUNTAIN LANDSCAPE

Pencil and watercolour, 37.5 × 28
Exhibited: *Charles Rennie Mackintosh, Margaret Macdonald Mackintosh, Memorial Exhibition*, McLellan Galleries, Glasgow 1933 (68)
Checklist number 69 [RB 197]
Private collection

38 VILLAGE IN THE MOUNTAINS

Pencil and watercolour, 37.5 × 28
Exhibited: *Charles Rennie Mackintosh, Margaret Macdonald Mackintosh, Memorial Exhibition*, McLellan Galleries, Glasgow 1933 (26)
Checklist number 70 [RB 196]
Private collection

A local architect, Bernard Catllar, has persuasively argued that these three watercolours [plates 36, 37 & 38] may have been conceived as a triptych recording the landscape facing Mont Louis. The two surviving works are identical in size, and butt together to create a view showing distinguishable mountain peaks, and the village, Planès de Dalt. M. Catllar speculates that the slightly smaller missing watercolour [plate 36] may show the left-hand part of the panorama, containing the Pic Gallinas.

FLOWERS

Mackintosh had drawn plant forms throughout his life. Initially they appeared as pencil studies interspersed between the pages of architectural jottings in his travel sketchbooks. The same analytical eye that scrutinised the construction, plans and sections of campanile, jambs and cornices, recorded and deconstructed the forms of nature. Gradually the studies became more sophisticated, though still confined to the pages of a sketchbook. Washes of pure watercolour were applied and increasingly complex patterns were made out of the tracery outlines of the plants. Dates, place names and his initials, often with those of Margaret Macdonald, were incorporated into cartouche boxes. During the years in London floral imagery emerged in rich profusion. Mackintosh produced vibrant textile designs, jazzy bouquets and a series of highly accomplished, gloriously coloured still-life paintings.

In France he lived surrounded by an abundance of beautiful wild flora. In the early spring, a burst of blossom, in particular the widely cultivated cherry, would make a spectacular show around Port Vendres. Some is shown in *A Spanish Farm* [plate 7] and *Summer in the South* [plate 8]. *The Chronycle* contains frequent references to the local flora: the apple tree in the 'Enchanted Valley' which was a favourite spot to sit and read, the cistus and tamarind trees, and the vivid ginesta. 'The Genesta is wonderful – it is perfectly amazing the perfume and the virgin clarity of the yellow colour.' (25 May, 7.4) And yet, remarkably few French botanical studies are known, and all but one are from Mont Louis, which offered a 'fairyland of flowers'. Perhaps the limited commercial success of the London still lifes, the absence of a studio, a declining interest in sketching, and the draw of new subjects in the surrounding landscape, contributed to the diminution in this side of his work. It had after all been a long-term diminution; Mackintosh's last known botanical study had been made in 1919.

Mimosa and *Pine Cones* returned to the format of the early 1900s: presenting elements of single specimens, in isolation, set against a plain background, in a manner which evoked the scientific botanical tradition of the eighteenth century. What is new in France is the mixed bouquet. With these Mackintosh celebrated the area's diversity of native plants, using the format of the stylised bouquets he had developed in London. What is also different is the greater freedom with which he recorded the plants. His earlier studies of single specimens demonstrate a sound botanical knowledge. The mixed groupings are less easy to identify, and at times show discrepancies of detail and scale, suggesting Mackintosh's focus was more on the decorative qualities of the varied groupings.

39 MIMOSA, AMÉLIE-LES-BAINS

Signed, dated and inscribed:
MYMOSA / AMELIE / LES-BAINS / JANUARY / 1924 / CRM.MMM
Pencil and watercolour, 25.7 × 21
Checklist number 71 [RB 203]
Hunterian Art Gallery, University of Glasgow

This is probably one of the first watercolours made in France. Mimosa is a spring-flowering plant. *Acacia dealbata* is the florist's mimosa and is a common adornment of Mediterranean gardens. Its native territory is south-east Australia and Tasmania.

MYMOSA
AMELIE
LES ◦ BAINS
JANUARY
1 9 2 4
CRM. MMM

40 DIANTHUS, MONT LOUIS

Signed, dated and inscribed:
DIANTHUS / MONT / LOUIS / JULY 1925 / MMM CRM
Pencil and watercolour, 25.3 × 19.9
Exhibited: *Charles Rennie Mackintosh, Margaret Macdonald Mackintosh, Memorial Exhibition*, McLellan Galleries, Glasgow 1933 (ex-cat.)
Not exhibited [PR 14]
National Gallery of Canada

This striking study contains at least eleven species, not all identifiable, but including pansy/violet, campion and knapweed. The title derives from the dianthus – carnation/pink – flowers which surround the cartouche and are shown both as an enlarged bloom, with shredded pink petals, and in profile at the top of the composition. Other flowers such as the viola at bottom left are also considerably enlarged. An unusual element is the black background, a device Mackintosh had used in his London textile designs and stylised bouquets. Its presence helps to unify the disparate elements and intensify the effect of the colours.

DIANTHUS
MONT
LOUIS
JULY 1925
MMM C RM

41 MIXED FLOWERS, MONT LOUIS

Signed, dated and inscribed:
MONT / LOUIS / JULY 1925 / MMM / CRM
Pencil and watercolour, 26.2 × 20.5
Exhibited: *Charles Rennie Mackintosh, Margaret Macdonald Mackintosh, Memorial Exhibition*, McLellan Galleries, Glasgow 1933 (87)
Checklist number 72 [RB 207]
The British Museum, London

The bouquet contains a rich array of almost twenty species, including forget-me-not, cornflower, willow herb, pinks, bellflower, pansies/ violets, and crane's bill. Mackintosh has also included a visual joke. At the top left is a species of yellow rattle. Mackintosh has rendered its flowers into birds' heads by adapting the distinctive dark markings of the tips of its petals into bills and eyes.

MONT
LOUIS
JULY 1925
MMM
CRM

42 MIXED FLOWERS, MONT LOUIS

Signed, dated and inscribed: MONT / LOUIS / JULY / 1925 / MMM CRM
Pencil and watercolour (dimensions unrecorded)
Not exhibited [PR 16]
Untraced (sold Christie's Glasgow, 18 December 1980, lot 10)

At least eight species appear to be recorded here, including daisy, carnation/pink, and a member of the figwort or mint family (centre left). The rest are not identifiable with any certainty.

43 MONT LOUIS, FLOWER STUDY

Signed, dated and inscribed: MONT LOUIS / 1925 / CRM MMM
Pencil and watercolour, 25.8 × 20.2
Not exhibited [RB 205]
Untraced (sold Christie's London, 17 February 1994, lot 77)

The central Martagon lily is surrounded by examples of (clockwise from below right) St John's wort, bellflowers, unidentified, knapweed, an example of the figwort or mint family, and sheep's bit (top right). The lily flower is, inaccurately, shown attached to the bellflower stem at the left.

MONT LOUIS
1 9 2 5
CRM MMM

44 PINE CONES, MONT LOUIS

Dated and inscribed: MONT / LOUIS / 1925
Pencil and watercolour, 26.9 × 20.8
Checklist number 73 [RB 206]
Hunterian Art Gallery, University of Glasgow

Black or Austrian pine (*Pinus nigra*), almost certainly the subject, is indigenous in southern Europe and is commonly planted there and elsewhere.

MONT
LOUIS
1925

CHRONOLOGY

This brief chronology lists the known publication and exhibition dates of Mackintosh's sketches and paintings up to 1933 and the first significant display of the French watercolours, at the *Mackintosh Memorial Exhibition*. For fuller biographies see Crawford and Kaplan, cited in the bibliography.

1868 Charles Rennie Mackintosh, born 7 June

1883 Registered as an evening student at Glasgow School of Art, until 1894.

1884 Joined John Hutchison, architect, Glasgow

1889 Joined Honeyman & Keppie, architects, Glasgow

1891 Sketches of Rome and Venice exhibited at the Glasgow School of Art Club Annual Exhibition

1892 *Palazzo Ca' d'Oro, Venice* and *Venetian Palace*, exhibited at the Glasgow Institute of Fine Arts

1893 *Central Doorway – Certosa di Pavia* and *Certosa di Pavia – Portion of Front*, exhibited at the Glasgow Institute of Fine Arts

1894 Italian sketches published in the *Glasgow Architectural Association Sketchbook*; *The Harvest Moon*, exhibited at the Glasgow Institute of Fine Arts

1893–6 Contributed watercolours to *The Magazine*, an album of students' work

1895 Nineteen English sketches published in the *British Architect* (44), November

1896 *Part Seen Imagined Part*, exhibited at the Arts and Crafts Exhibition Society, London

1898 *Princess Ess* and *Princess Uty*, exhibited at the Royal Society of Scottish Painters in Watercolours, Edinburgh

1899 *Princess Uty* exhibited at the Venice Biennale; *Princess Ess*, exhibited at the Glasgow Institute of Fine Arts; *The Black Thorn* and *The Moss* Rose exhibited at the International Society of Sculptors, Painters and Gravers, London

1900 *Princess Ess*, *Princess Uty*, *Whether the Roses be your Lips* and *The Tree of Death* exhibited at the Vienna Secession

C.R. Mackintosh married Margaret Macdonald

1901 C.R. Mackintosh became a partner in Honeyman & Keppie architects

1913 Partnership of Honeyman, Keppie & Mackintosh dissolved

1914 *Le Jardin*, exhibited at Les Arts Décoratifs de Grande-Bretagne et d'Irelande, Paris

Left Glasgow for Walberswick, Suffolk, and produced a series of some thirty botanical studies and a group of landscape paintings

1915 Moved to London

1916 *The Voices of the Wood*, a collaborative work with Margaret Macdonald, of oil paintings and candelabra, exhibited at the Arts and Crafts Exhibition Society, London; *Anemones* exhibited at the International Society of Sculptors, Painters and Gravers, London

1917 *Petunias* exhibited at the International Society of Sculptors, Painters and Gravers, London

1918 *Begonias* exhibited at the International Society of Sculptors, Painters and Gravers, London

1920 *Anemones* and *Petunias* exhibited at the British Arts and Crafts Exhibition, Detroit

1922 *The Road from the Ferry* exhibited at the 2nd International Exhibition of Watercolor Paintings, Chicago

1923 *A Landscape Panel* included in Exhibition of Decorative Art, 48th Royal Academy Winter Exhibition, London; *Pinks* and *The Grey Iris* exhibited at the Goupil Gallery, London; *Venetian Palace, Blackshore-on-the-Blyth* exhibited at the Royal Academy, London; *White Roses* exhibited at the 3rd International Exhibition of Watercolor Paintings, Chicago

Left London for France. Establishing a chronology for the subsequent years in France is difficult, as only a few of the watercolours are dated: *Mimosa, Amélie-les-Bains*, 1924; a group of four flowers drawings, from Mont Louis, all dated 1925; *La Rue du Soleil*, Port Vendres, dated twice – 1926 and 1927; *Le Fort Maillert, The Little Bay* and *The Rock*, all Port Vendres, 1927. Other destinations documented by the watercolours include the fishing village of Collioure, the valley towns of Ille-sur-Têt, Palalda and Bouleternère, and the mountain villages of Fetges and La Llagonne. It seems probable that by 1925 the Mackintoshes had established a routine of summering in Mont Louis, and spending the rest of the year on the coast at Port Vendres.

1923–4 Winter, spent at Amélie-les-Bains

1924 Spring, spent at Collioure and/or Port Vendres

Yellow Tulips exhibited at the 4th International Exhibition of Watercolor Paintings, Chicago

September to November, spent five weeks in London

1924–5 December to May, spent at Ille-sur-Têt

1925 June to July, spent at Mont Louis

Autumn, possibly spent at Ille-sur-Têt and/or Montpellier

The Grey Iris exhibited at the 5th International Exhibition of Watercolor Paintings, Chicago

1925–6 Winter, spent at Port Vendres

1926 March, possibly spent at Port Vendres

Collioure exhibited at the 6th International Exhibition of Watercolor Paintings, Chicago

1927 *Le Fort Mauresque*, exhibited at the British Artists' Exhibition, Galérie Georges Petit, Paris

Summer probably spent at Mont Louis

Returned to London

1928 *Fetges* exhibited at the Society of Scottish Painters, Edinburgh. *La Rue du Soleil* and *The Little Bay* sold by The Leicester Galleries, London

C.R. Mackintosh died, 10 December, in London

1933 Margaret Macdonald Mackintosh died, 7 January, in London

Mackintosh Memorial Exhibition, 4–27 May, McLellan Galleries, Glasgow

MAPS

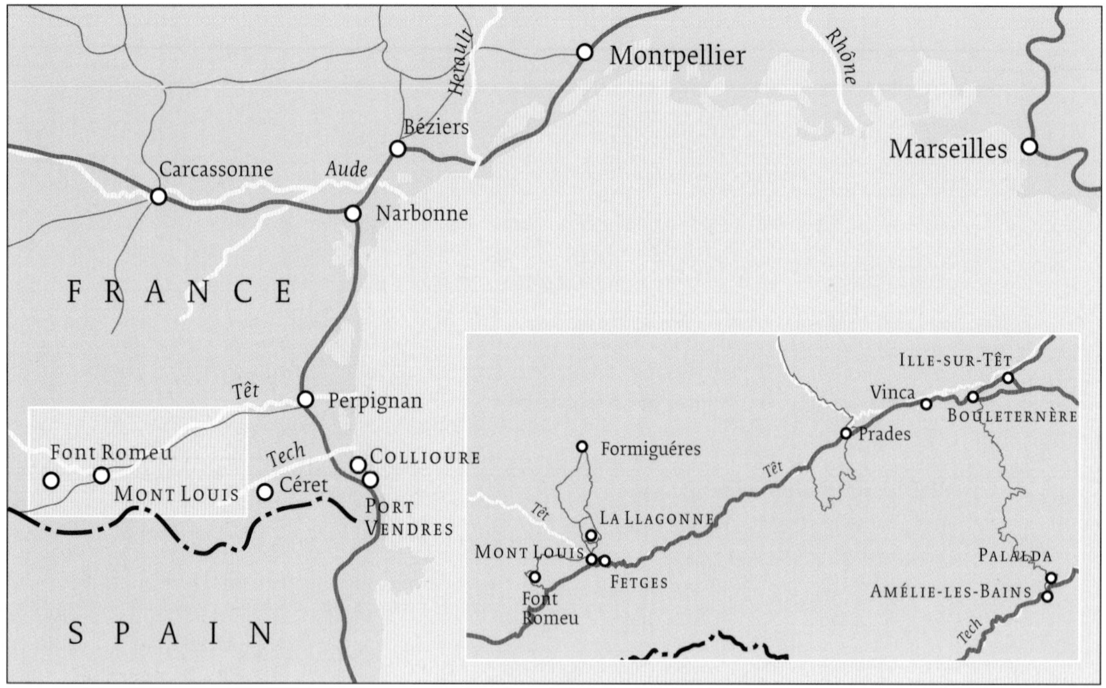

The Roussillion
This map shows the principal towns visited by the Mackintoshes between 1924 and 1927. Those places where Mackintosh painted are named in capitals.

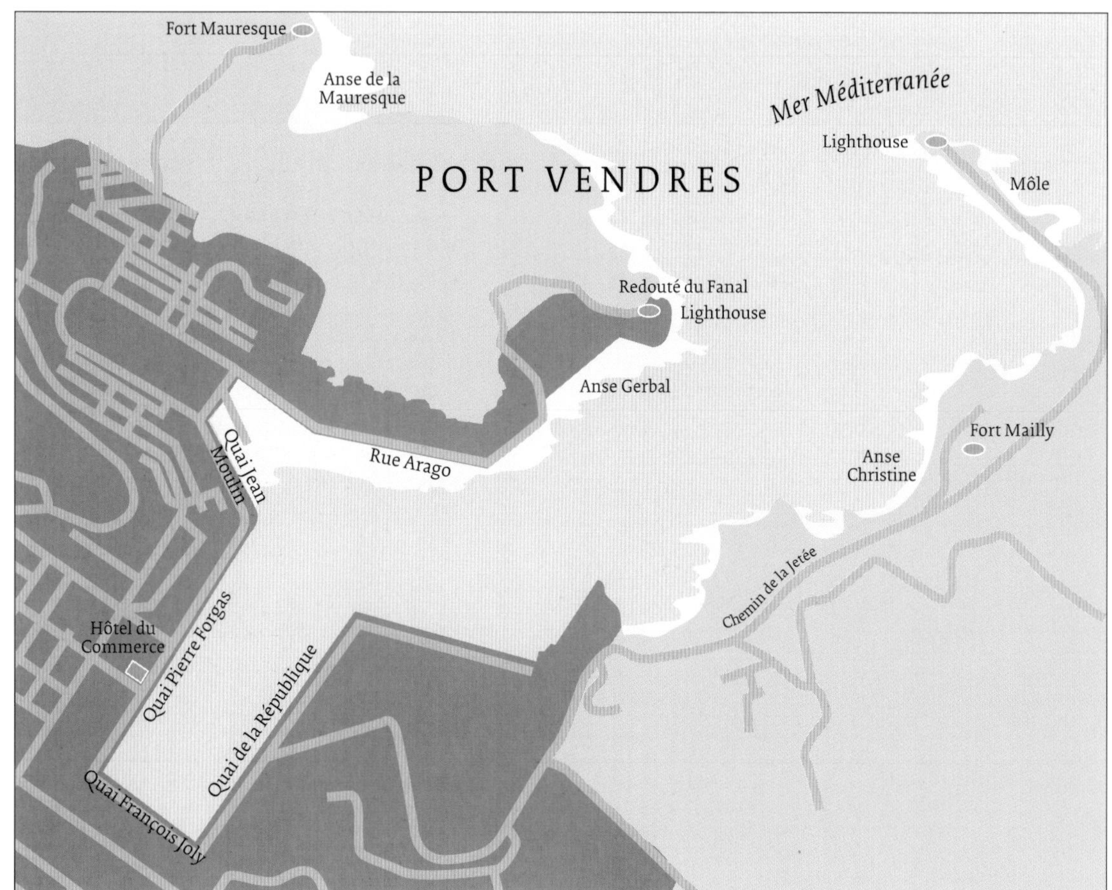

Port Vendres
The plan shows the main locations painted by Mackintosh and referred to in *The Chronycle*.

EXHIBITION CHECKLIST

All works are on paper. Dimensions are given in centimetres, height × width.

SCOTLAND, ITALY, ENGLAND 1880s–1923

1 *Cast of an Antique Relief* c.1886
Sepia, 72.4 × 54.6
Hunterian Art Gallery, University of Glasgow

2 *Sketchbook: Drawings of Architecture in Scotland* c.1888–1900
Pencil, 13.5 × 18
National Library of Ireland
Illustrated fig.11

3 *Tomb, Glasgow Cathedral* c.1889
Watercolour, 31.7 × 24.1
Hunterian Art Gallery, University of Glasgow

4 *Sketchbook: Drawings of Building Construction (details)* c.1890
Pencil and watercolour, 13.3 × 18.2
Hunterian Art Gallery, University of Glasgow

5 *Glasgow Cathedral at Sunset* dated 1890
Pencil and watercolour, 39.3 × 28.4
Hunterian Art Gallery, University of Glasgow
Illustrated fig.14

6 *Porlock Weir* mid-1890s
Pencil and watercolour, 26.6 × 41.2
Hunterian Art Gallery, University of Glasgow
Illustrated fig.16

7 *Sketchbook: Drawings of Architecture in Scotland and Italy* c.1888–1891
Pencil and watercolour, 12.6 × 17.6
National Library of Ireland

8 *Orvieto Cathedral* dated 1891
Pencil and watercolour, 31.8 × 24.2
Hunterian Art Gallery, University of Glasgow

9 *Blind Window, Certosa di Pavia* dated 1891
Pencil and watercolour, 67.5 × 38
Glasgow School of Art

10 *Mosaics, S. Apollinare Nuovo, Ravenna* May-June 1891
Pencil and watercolour, 43.3 × 33.3
Hunterian Art Gallery, University of Glasgow

11 *Sketchbook: Drawings of a Tour to Italy, France and Belgium* 1891
Pencil, 23.1 × 16.2
Glasgow School of Art

12 *Sketchbook: Drawings of Architecture in England* 1894
Pencil, 11.5 × 17.8
Hunterian Art Gallery, University of Glasgow

13 *Sketchbook: Drawings of Architecture and Plants in Scotland and England* c.1894–1910
Pencil, 11.4 × 17.2
Hunterian Art Gallery, University of Glasgow

14 *Dunginess, Bridport* c.1895
Pencil, 25.8 × 20.3
Hunterian Art Gallery, University of Glasgow

15 *Roof Bosses, Whitchurch* c.1895
Pencil and watercolour, 25.8 × 20.3
Hunterian Art Gallery, University of Glasgow

16 *Sketchbook: Drawings of Plants* c.1895
Pencil, 17.7 × 12.7
National Library of Ireland

17 *Sketchbook: Drawings of Architecture in England* c.1896–1901
Pencil, 13.4 × 18.5
Hunterian Art Gallery, University of Glasgow

18 *Castle, Holy Island* 1901
Pencil and watercolour, 20.3 × 26
Hunterian Art Gallery, University of Glasgow
Illustrated fig.12

19 *Barn, Saxlingham* dated 1905
Pencil, 20.1 × 25.7
Hunterian Art Gallery, University of Glasgow

20 *Well, Penha Verde, Cintra* dated June 1908
Pencil and watercolour, 25.8 × 20.1
Hunterian Art Gallery, University of Glasgow

21 *Sketchbook: Drawings of Architecture and Plants in England* 1897–1910
Pencil, 17.7 × 22.8
Hunterian Art Gallery, University of Glasgow

22 *Venetian Palace, Blackshore-on-the-Blyth* dated 1914
Watercolour, 41 × 56.4
Hunterian Art Gallery, University of Glasgow
Illustrated fig.19

23 *Walberswick* dated 1914
Watercolour, 28 × 38.2
Private collection
Illustrated fig.20

24 *Petunia, Walberswick* dated 1914
Pencil and watercolour, 25.8 × 20.2
Hunterian Art Gallery, University of Glasgow

25 *Fritillaria, Walberswick* dated 1915
Pencil and watercolour, 25.3 × 20.2
Hunterian Art Gallery, University of Glasgow

26 *Hazel Tree, Lamb's Tails, Walberswick* dated 1915
Pencil and watercolour, 27.8 × 20.7
Hunterian Art Gallery, University of Glasgow

27 *Japanese Witch Hazel, Walberswick* dated 1915
Pencil and watercolour, 26.3 × 21.1
Hunterian Art Gallery, University of Glasgow

28 *Textile Design: Basket of Flowers* c.1915–20
Watercolour, 31.7 × 30
Hunterian Art Gallery, University of Glasgow
Illustrated fig.37

29 *Begonias* dated 1916
Pencil and watercolour, 42.5 × 37.3
Private collection
Illustrated fig.40

30 *Design for an advertising label for Bassett-Lowke Ltd* c.1919
Pencil and watercolour, 26.2 × 20.5
Hunterian Art Gallery, University of Glasgow

31 *Design for an advertising label for Bassett-Lowke Ltd* c.1919
Pencil and watercolour, 26.2 × 20.5
Hunterian Art Gallery, University of Glasgow

32 *Advertising label for Bassett-Lowke Ltd* c.1919
Lithograph on paper, 6.4 × 4.5
Hunterian Art Gallery, University of Glasgow
Illustrated fig.38

33 *Village, Worth Matravers* 1920
Watercolour, 46 × 56.9
Glasgow School of Art
Illustrated fig.21

34 *The Downs, Worth Matravers* 1920
Watercolour, 45.2 × 53.7
Glasgow School of Art
Illustrated fig.22

35 *Worth Matravers* 1920
Pencil, 20.3 × 25
Hunterian Art Gallery, University of Glasgow
Illustrated fig.23

36 *Worth Matravers* 1920
Pencil, 20.3 × 25
Hunterian Art Gallery, University of Glasgow
Illustrated fig.24

37 *Ships* c.1922
Watercolour, 20.3 × 29.7
Private collection
Illustrated p.20

FRANCE 1923–1927

For a note on dating see p.32

VALLEYS AND HILLS

38 *Palalda, Pyrénées-Orientales*
Pencil and watercolour, 51.5 × 51.5
Private collection, on loan to the Scottish National Gallery of Modern Art, Edinburgh
Illustrated plate 1

39 *Bouleternère*
Pencil and watercolour, 44.7 × 44.7
Donald and Eleanor Taffner, New York
Illustrated plate 2

40 *Héré-de-Mallet, Ille-sur-Têt*
Pencil and watercolour, 46 × 46
Private collection, on loan to the Scottish National Gallery of Modern Art, Edinburgh
Illustrated plate 3

41 *A Hill Town in Southern France*
Pencil and watercolour, 42 × 42
Private collection
Illustrated plate 4

FARMHOUSES

42 *Mont Alba*
Pencil and watercolour, 38.7 × 43.8
Scottish National Gallery of Modern Art, Edinburgh, purchased 1990
Illustrated plate 5

43 *Blanc Ontoine*
Pencil and watercolour, 39.1 × 50.6
Hunterian Art Gallery, University of Glasgow
Illustrated plate 6

44 *A Spanish Farm*
Pencil and watercolour, 28 × 38
Private collection
Illustrated plate 7

45 *Summer in the South*
Pencil and watercolour, 28.3 × 38.5
Private collection, on loan to the Scottish National Gallery of Modern Art, Edinburgh
Illustrated plate 8

46 *A Southern Farm*
Pencil and watercolour, 43.4 × 43.4
Hunterian Art Gallery, University of Glasgow
Illustrated plate 9

COLLIOURE

47 *Collioure, Pyrénées-Orientales – Summer Palace of the Queens of Aragon*
Pencil and watercolour, 38.1 × 43.2
The National Trust for Scotland, The Hill House
Illustrated plate 10

48 *Collioure*
Pencil and watercolour, 39.7 × 46.5
The Art Institute of Chicago, Suzanne Searle Dixon Endowment; gift of Mrs Herbert Vance; Margaret Day Blake; Olivia Shaler Swan, Print & Drawing Fund, Sara R. Shorey, Mr and Mrs David C. Hilliard, Stanley Field, Mr and Mrs William Hunt, William McCallin McKee Memorial, Joseph Ryerson, Mary S. Adams, Elizabeh Gott Templeton, Everett D. Graff, Henry H. Huxley, Robert M. Chase, and Print and Drawing Endowments; Print and Drawing Purchase Fund.
Illustrated plate 11

49 *A Southern Town*
Pencil and watercolour, 32.3 × 37.5
Hunterian Art Gallery, University of Glasgow
Illustrated plate 12

PORT VENDRES

50 *A Southern Port*
Pencil and watercolour, 36.2 × 44.5
Glasgow Museums: Kelvingrove Art Gallery and Museum
Illustrated plate 13

51 *Port Vendres*
Pencil and watercolour, 28 × 39.6
The British Museum, London
Illustrated plate 14

52 *Port Vendres, La Ville*
Pencil and watercolour, 46 × 46
Glasgow Museums: Kelvingrove Art Gallery and Museum
Illustrated plate 15

53 *La Rue du Soleil* dated 1927; dated verso 1926
Pencil and watercolour, 39.7 × 38.2
Hunterian Art Gallery, University of Glasgow
Illustrated plate 16

54 *The Little Bay, Port Vendres* dated 1927
Pencil and watercolour, 39.3 × 39.3
Hunterian Art Gallery, University of Glasgow
Illustrated plate 17

55 *Men Unloading a Steamer at the Quayside*
Crayon and watercolour, 25.3 × 21.1
Hunterian Art Gallery, University of Glasgow
Illustrated plate 18

56 *Steamer Moored at the Quayside*
Crayon and watercolour, 25.3 × 21.1
Hunterian Art Gallery, University of Glasgow
Illustrated plate 19

57 *Steamer at the Quayside*
Crayon and watercolour, 25.2 × 21
Hunterian Art Gallery, University of Glasgow
Illustrated plate 20

58 *Steamers at the Quayside*
Crayon and watercolour, 25.2 × 21
Hunterian Art Gallery, University of Glasgow
Illustrated plate 21

59 *The Lighthouse*
Pencil and watercolour, 27 × 37.5
Private collection, courtesy of The Fine Art Society, London
Illustrated plate 23

60 *The Fort*
Pencil and watercolour, 45.2 × 45.4
Hunterian Art Gallery, University of Glasgow
Illustrated plate 25

61 *Le Fort Maillert* dated 1927
Pencil and watercolour, 35.8 × 28.5
Glasgow School of Art
Illustrated plate 26

62 *Port Vendres*
Pencil and watercolour, 28.8 × 39.6
Private collection, courtesy of The Fine Art Society, London
Illustrated plate 27

63 *The Rock* dated 1927
Pencil and watercolour, 30.5 × 36.8
Private collection
Illustrated plate 28

MOUNTAINS

64 *Slate Roofs*
Pencil and watercolour, 37 × 27.8
Glasgow School of Art
Illustrated plate 29

65 *Fetges*
Pencil and watercolour, 46.5 × 45.8
Tate: presented by Walter W. Blackie 1929
Illustrated plate 30

66 *The Boulders*
Pencil and watercolour, 33.3 × 38
Hunterian Art Gallery, University of Glasgow
Illustrated plate 32

67 *The Village of La Llagonne*
Pencil and watercolour, 45.7 × 45.7 cm
Glasgow Museums: Kelvingrove Art Gallery and Museum
Illustrated plate 34

68 *The Church of La Llagonne*
Pencil and watercolour, 28 × 38.3
Private collection
Illustrated plate 35

69 *Mountain Landscape*
Pencil and watercolour, 37.5 × 28
Private collection
Illustrated plate 37

70 *Village in the Mountains*
Pencil and watercolour, 37.5 × 28
Private collection
Illustrated plate 38

FLOWERS

71 *Mimosa, Amélie-les-Bains* dated January 1924
Pencil and watercolour, 25.7 × 21
Hunterian Art Gallery, University of Glasgow
Illustrated plate 39

72 *Mixed Flowers, Mont Louis* dated July 1925
Pencil and watercolour, 26.2 × 20.5
The British Museum, London
Illustrated plate 41

73 *Pine Cones, Mont Louis* dated 1925
Pencil and watercolour, 26.9 × 20.8
Hunterian Art Gallery, University of Glasgow
Illustrated plate 44

These three letters, recently acquired by the Hunterian Art Gallery, University of Glasgow, are previously unpublished. The transcriptions have retained Macdonald's punctuation, which favoured dashes to commas or full stops, and the occasional spelling lapse.

LETTER 1

La Petite Maison Bouix.
Amélie-les-Bains
Pyrénées-Orientales
South France. [December 1923]

My dear Jessie.
This is our address just now – + will be for the next two months – I expect you will have heard from the Hutchies that we were intending to come[1] – We should so much like to have seen you + Mr Newbery – but I expect you were very much rushed[2] – We were so glad to hear that you were both looking so well – It would have been nice to have heard about all your experiences in Spain. I suppose it was very lovely – we are really more like Spain here than France – the people are quite a Spanish type + all wear dead black + speak Catalan amongst themselves – altho' they understand French – We have taken this tiny house – it has just two rooms – one on the top of the other (+ I think must have been the old Toll-house) for studios + we are living at the little hotel just across the bridge – at one end of which this house stands. The hotel is simple – but beautifully clean + the cooking amazing + is very cheap – so that suits us.

I have let my studio furnished – but Toshie has / not yet let his – but we have left it in the hands of an Agent – so I expect it will let – but there is evidently not such a demand for studios as there was – artists are demanding more comfort + a lot prefer to take floors in big houses – where they get big rooms + a bathroom – rather than put up with the discomforts of studios like ours even tho' very picturesque – moreover – the rents are now doubled + are really too high for such studios I have been thinking for some time that we were foolish to go on with them. However, till we return + decide what is best to do – it is better to let them furnished.[3]

This is quite a beautiful spot – in the valley of the Tech – so we are sheltered from the Tramontane – but we get the snow-wind off Canigou if the wind blows from her direction – This, in spite of the glorious sun always gives a sharpness to the air which is rather exhilarating. Later on – in the Spring we think of going down to Colliure [*sic*] – We went to see how we liked it + think it is one of the most wonderful places we have ever seen – It is only a fishing village + it will be difficult to find accommodation – as there is no hotel – but I expect we shall manage somehow.

It seems a far cry from here to Worth Matravers[4] – but so far we always say we have not yet seen anything quite so perfect – I suppose you often walk out? The only thing that tempts one abroad (besides the exchange) is the certainty of fine weather – it does make such a difference to know it will be fine. Of course there is the other side to the picture. At Collioure – they have had no rain for two years – so water is rather precious. Here there is no lack – both drinking + boiling sulphur water – the latter simply flows down the street gutter + one can always get a can of beautiful hot water without the trouble of heating – It is lovely for washing – especially one's hair. Well – as I shall not write again before Christmas – I just wanted you to know where we were – we send you all good wishes for a Merry Christmas + a very Happy New Year with best love

Yours affectionately
Margaret M. Mackintosh.

LETTER 2

Hotel du Midi
Amélie-les-Bains
Pyrénées-Orientales.
South France. Dec. 18. 1924

My dear Jessie.
Here we are – back again in our beloved Pyrénées – We went back to Chelsea in September – intending to stay in London perhaps till January + then return here – but strange to say – the studios, this year, let almost at once – + each tenant wanted to get in at once – so we just had a very short stay in Chelsea of five weeks. Last year – we had such a difficulty letting the studios – that I thought it better to take the chance when we had it for altho' we find we cannot let them – so as to make anything off them – which seems – rather strange – still we get the rent we pay for them back so do not need to worry.

We like life here so much + Toshie is as / as happy as a sandboy – tremendously interested in his painting + of course doing some remarkable work. I hope he will have a show sometime – but that remains to be seen about – when he has got enough work together. In the meantime – he is absorbed in this landscape – since we got here on Nov. 22. he has been able to work outside every day but 2 – from 9.30 till three – in brilliant sunshine – I don't work outside – but it is warm enough to sit indoors –without a fire. We intend to stay in Ille till the end of March anyway. It is a charming place + the little hotel most comfortable we live – the two of us for 8/- a day wine included.

We left London on Nov. 2 + went Folkestone – Boulogne + then to Montreuil-sur-Mer to see the little town + the Macauley-Stevenson. Stansmore got us lodging with the mother of her servant + we were most comfortable. We spent most of our time with the Macauleys + had a very good time They were most kind to us + they have made a charming dwelling for themselves + both seem very happy + contented – Macauley has hardly altered at all + Stansmore is only a little plumper – There is no doubt she is a perfect wife for Macauley + she has a wonderful influence over him just in the way in which he perhaps needs it a little – but there is no question he is a charming person + very entertaining + stimulating. He seems to do a lot of work + has some pictures in the studio which are very beautiful. We did not like the climate of Montreuil tho'. It is very like Winchelsea – a little hill town in a marshy plain + it was much too damp for our taste. When we left – the Stevensons + an American painter – one of the colony at Etaples – came to Paris with us – to see the Autumn Salon – which we found very interesting I liked especially the work of a man called Crotti[5] – he seemed to be doing what I have been trying to do all my life – but Macauley would not look at it – he disliked it so much – which / shows what an Ishmael I am! –

Then we came on here – to this lovely rose-colored land + we were glad to be back again in its warmth + sun. We find that prices are going up a little here – but they still take us – at this hotel for 8/- a day – both of us – wine included as we are going to stay some time – so there is not much to grumble about yet. London – I found dearer than ever – everything costs more + rents are getting absurd.

I heard from Gladys Owen – she tells me that the eldest Alexander girl + the eldest Priestman girl are engaged.[6]

I was very sorry to see about Mrs Gauler's [?] death. I know it would be a great grief to you – For her – the war made such a tragedy – that perhaps she would not mind.

I hope you are both well + happy. We both send our best love + every good wish.

Margaret M. Mackintosh

You saw of course that Revel of the Chelsea Poly. has got Glasgow. Schwabe thought Walter Bayes would get it – There seems to have been a lot in for it – including – to our amusement – Stuart Park + David Gauld[7] I think Macauley said that was private – so do not mention it – I can't see it matters tho' – we feel it does not matter much who gets it – No one will / ever again know how to run it like Fra H. Newbery. That's our opinion + we know – perhaps better than anyone! –

LETTER 3

Hôtel du Midi
Ille-sur-Tet
Pyrénées-Orientales
Jan. 23. 1925

My dear Jessie,
I am hastening to write – because I am afraid you may be uneasy not hearing. Your letter must have been held up in Amelie-les-Bains, while the dear people thought matters over. You directed it to Hotel du Midi, Amelie-les-Bains – We – when we left Amelie, asked the Post-office to forward letters for Mackintosh Hotel Pujade to Hotel du Midi Ille-sur-Tet. This was of course too much for the dear Catalans to decide about quickly they never do anything in a hurry – so they have evidently pondered it for 4 or 5 days before sending it on – So that is why you have not heard from me before. Now – of course – you really ought not to send us such a present – it is *far* too kind of you – However – we know you love to do it – even, as I always say – to the giving away of your head – if anyone you / you loved wanted it! – So we thank you very very much indeed for it. Toshie instantly decided upon his present – He has been longing to get a pair of, what they call here – mountain boots. ever since he saw them here. They are made of a lovely soft natural-colored leather – + so now – he is going to treat himself to a pair – I cannot yet think of anything I particularly want – just at the moment – but there is sure something to turn up + I shall buy it when it does –

Just now – I am enjoying influenza – Toshie has just finished his + has passed it on to me. It is very prevalent just now – they say the winter has been too warm. It has certainly been amazing. Since we came here at the end of Nov. we have had continual sunshine – except for two days tropical rain – we have not even had the winds which usually blow at this time – one day after another has been still. sunny / + blue.skyed – One cannot believe it when one reads of the weather in England. However – we may get it yet – the gardeners all live in hope of a little frost. They say it makes the worms do something to the earth which makes the salads good.

It will be very exciting to be building I think you are very wise to put in a bathroom. Quite apart from the joy of a hot bath – I believe it averts many an illness. Macauley had put in a most ingenuous bathroom in his house with a large sort of Kettle heated by gas. Jean – we did not see – because she has gone for a year, I think, to travel about with some friends who are now in Corsica. They pay all her expenses + she lends a hand with the children when required. They seem to be charming people – I forget their name – but they came some time ago to Etaples + bought a house there – which they tired of – so / they have let it + are now wandering about just as fancy takes them – Stansmore thinks it will be very jolly for Jean as they are bright young people, always making friends + the children are delightful + Jean writes of all sorts of jolly times she is having.

You think, as we do – about Dorset – It is quite the best in every way – this comes very near it + the buildings here are a perpetual joy to us. Toshie is going to paint some of the 'maas' as they call them – farmhouses really – so you will see what they are like some day – I hope.

When we come again to Corfe – we must make an excursion + see the panels at Bridport the Fra is doing. You are both, evidently, very well + enjoying life which is the best thing in the world, isn't it.

Best love to you both from us both + many many thanks

Yours affectionately
Margaret M. Mackintosh

NOTES AND REFERENCES

ABBREVIATIONS

The Chronycle: Pamela Robertson (ed.), *The Chronycle: The Letters of Charles Rennie Mackintosh to Margaret Macdonald Mackintosh 1927*, Hunterian Art Gallery, University of Glasgow, 2001. Mackintosh's occasional lapses of punctuation and spelling are repeated in the quotations.

CRM: Charles Rennie Mackintosh
MM: Margaret Macdonald Mackintosh
HAG: Hunterian Art Gallery, University of Glasgow

MACKINTOSH'S FRENCH WATERCOLOURS · PAGES 9–19

1 Hermann Muthesius, 'Mackintosh's Art Principles', *A House for an Art Lover*, Darmstadt: Alexander Koch, 1902.
2 See, for example, Isabel Savory, *The Romantic Roussillon*, London: Fisher Unwin, 1919 or Louis Charles Eugene Fouchier, *Un Mois aux Pyrénées*, Paris: Hachette, 1920
3 *Blue Guide to Southern France*, London and Paris, 1926, pp.382 & 436.
4 Amy Oakley, *Hill-Towns of the Pyrenees*, New York: The Century Company, 1923. MM's notes, HAG.
5 Mackintosh's loyal friend and patron, William Davidson, told Thomas Howarth that the painter John Lavery had lent the Mackintoshes his Spanish home, though there is no corroboratory evidence for this. See Notebook B, Howarth Archive, University of Toronto Archives, B2000-0002/030(25), p.24. Patrick Geddes (1854–1932), Scottish scientist, sociologist, town planner, philosopher and friend of the Mackintoshes from their Glasgow period, ran a Scots College in Montpellier. His daughter, Nora, and her husband, Frank Mears, visited the Mackintoshes in Ille-sur-Têt in 1925.
6 CRM to J.D. Fergusson, 1 February 1925 (Coll. unknown); CRM to Francis Newbery, 28 December 1925 (National Library of Scotland), both published in Alistair Moffat, *Remembering Charles Rennie Mackintosh*, Lanark: Colin Baxter, 1989 and *The Chronycle*.
7 The letters were given by Jessie's daughter, Mary, to Thomas Howarth. They were acquired by HAG, 2005, with support from the National Fund for Acquisitions and the Friends of the National Libraries. They are transcribed in the Appendix.
8 MM to Jessie Newbery, 18 December 1924.
9 MM to Jessie Newbery, [December 1923].
10 Ibid.
11 MM to Jessie Newbery, 18 December 1924.
12 Ibid.
13 MM to Jessie Newbery [December 1923].
14 W.S. Moyes, a draughtsman for the firm, described in a letter to Thomas Howarth how Mackintosh *was a very quick worker and never seemed to get tired. Most of the drawings for the various works were prepared by him, any assistance rendered by others being to sketches and information supplied. His usual method was to consider the problem and prepare a sketch on detail paper (obtained from a great roll larger than the rolls used for the production of newspapers). It was of good quality and the surface not rendered useless when a rubber was used. After sketches were considered and approved – plans, elevations, and sections were made on Whatman paper rough surface to scale of ⅛ in = 1 ft. Then if the nature of the design required more consideration, scale drawings of portions of external and internal work were made to scale of ½ in = 1 ft any departure being incorporated in the ⅛ in scale plans before being traced. He did the tracing himself frequently using a broad strong line, and the firm supplied all helios from their own plant. Sometimes he smoked a pipe as he worked at other times he would sing, a*

favourite being 'Tit Willow'. His palette consisted of less than twelve colours usually half or whole cakes, with a huge lump of gamboge [Gum resin from various east Asian trees used as yellow pigment]. 6 June 1947, Howarth Archive, University of Toronto Archives, B96-0028/017(13).

15 CRM 'Scotch Baronial Architecture' (1890), see Pamela Robertson (ed.), *Charles Rennie Mackintosh: The Architectural Writings*, Wendlebury: White Cockade, 1990, p.49.

16 CRM to Francis Newbery, 28 December 1925 (National Library of Scotland).

17 For a fuller account of Mackintosh's working practice, see *The Chronycle*, pp.24–9. *The Chronycle* charts his progress over a six-week period as he worked on at least four watercolours: *The Lighthouse*, *Port Vendres*, *Elephants* (a still-life subject), and *The Rock*.

18 The description of *The Rock* also makes reference to 'the reflection of the Rock', which does not form part of the surviving painting [plate 28].

19 Alan Crawford, *Charles Rennie Mackintosh*, London: Thames and Hudson, 1995, p.50–1.

A PAINTER AMONGST PAINTERS PAGES 21–29

1 Klaus Albrecht Schröder, 'Not Blind to the World', Klaus Albrecht Schröder and Harald Szeeman (ed.), *Egon Schiele and his Contemporaries - Austrian Painting and Drawing from 1900 to 1930 from the Leopold Collection, Vienna*, Munich 1988, p.24.

2 Roger Billcliffe and Peter Vergo, 'Charles Rennie Mackintosh and the Austrian Art Revival, *Burlington Magazine* 119 (November 1977), p.740.

3 14 May 1927, 3.1: 'The Ship that brought the gold dust...', *The Chronycle*, p.53.

4 11 June 1927, 15.3, ibid., p.90.

5 Quoted in Margaret Morris, *The Art of J.D. Fergusson: A Biased Biography*, Glasgow and London 1974, p.154.

6 9 June 1927, 14.1, *The Chronycle*, p.87.

7 Letter from Derain to Vlaminck, 25 June 1905, quoted in Patrick Elliott, 'Il fauvismo e il Midi', *L'Oro e l'Azzurro: I colori del Sud da Cézanne a Bonnard* (exhibition catalogue), Treviso, 2003.

8 19 June 1927, 20A, *The Chronycle*, p.96.

9 11 June 1927, 15.3, 8 June 1927 13.3, ibid., pp.90–1, p.86.

10 30 May 1927, 9.4, ibid., p.74.

11 7 June 1927, 10.2, ibid., pp.75–6.

12 8 June 1927, 14.1, 12 June 1927, 16.1, ibid., pp.86 & 92.

13 4 June 1927, 11.4 & footnote 99, ibid., p.79 for references to Mackintosh's friendship with Pryde.

14 30 May 1927, 9.4, ibid., p.74.

15 14 June 1927, 16.2, ibid., p.92.

16 7 June, 10.2, ibid., pp.75–6.

THE FRENCH WATERCOLOURS PAGES 31–109

1 Isabel Savory *The Romantic Roussillon* London: Unwin, 1919: pp. 56–7.

2 CRM to J.D. Fergusson, 1 February 1925 (National Library of Scotland).

3 H. Ormsby *France A Regional and Economic Geography* London: Methuen 1931, p.206.

4 MM to Jessie Newbery [December 1923] (HAG).

5 Isabel Savory, *The Romantic Roussillon*, London: T. Fisher Unwin, 1919, pp. 119–120.

6 Ibid., p.200.

APPENDIX · PAGES 116–17

1 W.O. Hutchison (1889–1970), Scottish painter resident in London, friend of the Mackintoshes from Glasgow days. His wife Margery was the daughter of the Scottish painter and another friend of the Mackintoshes', E.A. Walton (1860–1922).

2 Francis H. Newbery (1853–1946), Director of Glasgow School of Art from 1885 to 1917 and lifelong friend of the Mackintoshes. His wife Jessie Newbery (1864–1947) was a talented embroideress, designer and teacher. The couple retired to Corfe Castle, Dorset.

3 The Mackintoshes rented adjoining studios in London at 2 Cedar Studios, 45 Glebe Place and 2 Hans Studios, 43a Glebe Place.

4 Worth Matravers, Dorset. The Mackintoshes visited Worth at least once, in 1920, when Mackintosh painted two landscapes of the village. See figs.21 & 22.

5 Jean Crotti (1878–1958).

6 Miss Alexander, possibly a daughter of the Scottish painter, Edwin Alexander (1870–1926). Miss Priestman, daughter of the English painter Bertram Priestman (1868–1951).

7 Fra Newbery was succeeded as director at Glasgow School of Art by John Henderson, 1918–24. His successor was John D. Revel (1884–1967). Walter Bayes (1869–1956) was an English artist, illustrator and critic, who became Head of Westminster School of Art. James Stuart Park (1862–1933) and David Gauld (1865–1936) were both Glasgow-based painters.

SELECT BIBLIOGRAPHY

This select bibliography cites the principal texts in which Mackintosh's sketching and painting are discussed. For bibliographies of Mackintosh's other work as an architect and designer, see Howarth and Kaplan.

BILLCLIFFE, Roger, *Architectural Sketches & Flower Drawings by Charles Rennie Mackintosh*, London, 1977

BILLCLIFFE, Roger, *Mackintosh Watercolours*, London, 3rd edn, 1992

CRAWFORD, Alan, *Charles Rennie Mackintosh*, London, 1995

GROGAN, Elaine, *Beginnings: Charles Rennie Mackintosh's Early Sketches*, Dublin, 2002

HOWARTH, Thomas, *Charles Rennie Mackintosh and the Modern Movement*, London, 3rd edn, 1990

KAPLAN, Wendy (ed.), *Charles Rennie Mackintosh*, Glasgow and New York, 1996

ROBERTSON, Pamela (ed.), *Charles Rennie Mackintosh: The Architectural Papers*, Wendlebury, 1990

ROBERTSON, Pamela, *Charles Rennie Mackintosh: Art is the Flower*, London and New York, 1995

ROBERTSON, Pamela (ed.), *Charles Rennie Mackintosh Architectural Sketches*, Glasgow, 1999

ROBERTSON, Pamela (ed.), *The Chronycle: The Letters of Charles Rennie Mackintosh to Margaret Macdonald Mackintosh 1927*, Glasgow, 2001

COPYRIGHT AND PHOTOGRAPHIC CREDITS

AIC Photographic Service: p.20, fig. 40, plates 1,3, 5, 7, 8, 35, 37, 38
Annan Gallery, Glasgow: figs.1, 18, plates 3, 22, 31, 33
© The artist's estate: figs.39, 42
© The artist's family, courtesy of the Portland Gallery, London: figs. 43, 45
© Colin Baxter: p.42
© Christie's Images: plates 2, 4, 24, 42, 43
Alan Crawford: pp.32, 44, 52, 60, 64, 68, 82, 86, 92, 94
André Derain © ADAGP, Paris and DACS, London 2005: fig. 46
© The Fergusson Gallery, Perth and Kinross Council, Scotland: figs.41, 44
© The Fine Art Society, London / Bridgeman Art Library: plate 27
Hunterian Art Gallery, University of Glasgow: p.112
Philip Long: pp.34, 36, 54, 56, 62, 66, 74, 76, 78, 80